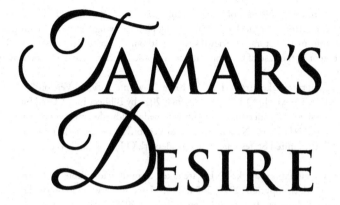

TAMAR'S DESIRE

Finding Hope, Encouragement, and
Strength in the Midst of Infertility

ANGIE HAGER

WESTBOW
PRESS®
A DIVISION OF THOMAS NELSON
& ZONDERVAN

WestBow Press books may be ordered through booksellers or by contacting:

WestBow Press
A Division of Thomas Nelson & Zondervan
1663 Liberty Drive
Bloomington, IN 47403
www.westbowpress.com
1 (866) 928-1240

ISBN: 978-1-9736-4182-7 (sc)
ISBN: 978-1-9736-4181-0 (hc)
ISBN: 978-1-9736-4183-4 (e)

Library of Congress Control Number: 2018911901

Print information available on the last page.

WestBow Press rev. date: 10/23/2018

To my husband, Tim, who has supported and encouraged me to write about "our story." I thank God every day that he blessed me with you as my life partner. Your godly leadership in our home has more God winks and miracles than I could ever imagine. Nothing—absolutely nothing—is impossible with God!

And to God Almighty, who nudged me to share our infertility story with the world. May he shine through these devotions and help strengthen one's faith that all things are possible through him.

Dear Reader,

Proverbs tells us that four things will never satisfy us. One of these four things is an empty womb. It's no wonder why millions of women in the United States have sought some fertility treatment. Infertility affects one in eight couples, but it is often treated in silence. *Tamar's Desire* shares more than fifty heart-wrenching devotions and shows how God is in control of every circumstance. I hope this devotional will be a guidebook that offers hope, encouragement, and perseverance for those suffering from infertility. May we see God in every circumstance of our lives—and may we continue to rely on him for strength.

Love,
Angie

GENESIS 38:1-27

At that time, Judah left his brothers and went down to stay with a man of Adullam named Hirah. There Judah met the daughter of a Canaanite man named Shua. He married her and made love to her; she became pregnant and gave birth to a son, who was named Er. She conceived again and gave birth to a son and named him Onan. She gave birth to still another son and named him Shelah. It was at Kezib that she gave birth to him.

Judah got a wife for Er, his firstborn, and her name was Tamar. But Er, Judah's firstborn, was wicked in the Lord's sight; so the Lord put him to death. Then Judah said to Onan, "Sleep with your brother's wife and fulfill your duty to her as a brother-in-law to raise up offspring for your brother." But Onan knew that the child would not be his; so whenever he slept with his brother's wife, he spilled semen on the ground to keep from providing offspring for his brother. What he did was wicked in the Lord's sight; so the Lord put him to death also.

Judah then said to his daughter-in-law Tamar, "Live as a widow in your father's household until my son Shelah grows up." For he thought, "He may die too, just like his brothers." So Tamar went to live in her father's household.

After a long time Judah's wife, the daughter of Shua, died. When Judah had recovered from his grief, he went up to Timnah, to the men who were shearing his sheep, and his friend Hirah the Adullamite went with him. When Tamar was told, "Your father-in-law is on his way to Timnah, to shear his sheep," she took off her widow's clothes, covered herself with a veil to disguise herself, and then sat down at the entrance to Enaim, which is on the road to Timnah. For she saw that, though Shelah had now grown up, she had not been given to him as a wife.

When Judah saw her, he thought she was a prostitute, for she had covered her face. Not realizing that she was his daughter-in-law, he went over to her by the roadside and said, "Come now, let me sleep with you."

"And what will you give me to sleep with you?" she asked.

"I'll send you a young goat from my flock," he said.

"Will you give me something else as a pledge until you send it?" she asked.

He said, "What pledge should I give you?"

"Your seal and its cord, and the staff in your hand," she answered. So he gave them to her and slept with her, and she became pregnant by him. After she left, she took off her veil and put on her widow's clothes again.

Meanwhile Judah sent the young goat by his friend the Adullamite in order to get his pledge back from the woman, but he did not find her. He asked the men who lived there, "Where is the shrine prostitute who was beside the road at Enaim?"

"There hasn't been any shrine prostitute here," they said.

So he went back to Judah and said, "I didn't find her. Besides, the men who lived there said, 'There hasn't been any shrine prostitute here.'"

Then Judah said, "Let her keep what she has or we will become a laughingstock. After all, I did send her this young goat, but you didn't find her."

About three months later Judah was told, "Your daughter-in-law Tamar is guilty of prostitution, and as a result she is now pregnant."

Judah said, "Bring her out and have her burned to death!"

As she was being brought out, she sent a message to her father-in-law. "I am pregnant by the man who owns these," she said. And she added, "See if you recognize whose seal and cord and staff these are."

Judah recognized them and said, "She is more righteous than I, since I wouldn't give her to my son Shelah." And he did not sleep with her again. When the time came for her to give birth, there were twin boys in her womb.

CONTENTS

CHOICES

FIFTY BEATS

I CAN'T GET NO SATISFACTION

THE MIRACLE OF LIFE

APPLES, ORANGES & BANANAS

JUST THE TWO OF US

OUT OF MY HANDS

"For I know the plans I have for you," declares
the Lord, "plans to prosper you and not to harm
you, plans to give you a hope and a future."
—Jeremiah 29:11

Have you ever played the game Life? The board game attempts to represent the life events of a person, such as going to school, raising a family, working, buying a home, having a child, and retiring. A spin of the wheel determines the future. The game contains various crossroads where a player can choose to go in one direction or another. Each path ultimately leads to the winning space, although different choices in the game lead to different results along the way.

In my game of life, I married, bought a home, and had a great job, but the babies never came. Months turned to years, and I was still not pregnant. My life path was not going as I had anticipated. It felt like I was losing.

But God had a plan for my life. He knew the direction it was going to take. Before his plan could take place, I had to learn a few lessons. I had to learn about myself. I had to learn about marriage, and most importantly, I had to learn to rely on God through all circumstances. I had to give God the reins of my entire life—not just a portion of it. All of it.

Are you pushing plans on God? He does not need our help.

He already has our lives figured out. His plan is far greater than we could ever imagine. So, get ready, get set, and go!

~

Dear God,

Thank you for creating my future. Your plans are far better than I could ever imagine, and I do not want to miss them by being consumed with my agenda. Please help me trust you with all things. Amen.

WHAT DO YOU THINK?

*W*here are you in your game of life?

*H*ow can you give your plans over to God?

A CLASS OF OUR OWN

> To the woman he said, "I will make your pains in childbearing
> very severe; with painful labor you will give birth to children."
> —Genesis 3:16

After the fall of sin, God curses women with painful labor. The
curse also includes pain in conceiving children. It is no surprise
then why we read about so many biblical accounts of infertility.
Genesis shares the story of Abraham and Sarah and the promise
God made by giving them a son, Isaac, at a very old age. The Bible
also tells the story of Isaac and Rebekah's struggle. Scripture says
that Isaac pleaded with God on behalf of his wife because she was
unable to have children.

Jacob, Isaac's son, and his wife, Rachel, battled infertility.

> When Rachel saw that she was not bearing Jacob
> any children, she became jealous of her sister. So
> she said to Jacob, "Give me children or I'll die!"
> (Genesis 30:1).

Each of the three great biblical patriarchs—Abraham, Isaac,
and Jacob—had wives who had difficulty conceiving. The Bible
also tells the story of Hannah, who struck a bargain with God to
have a son. There is Tamar, who prostituted herself for a child,

and Elizabeth, the cousin of Mary, who conceived when she least expected it.

Today is no different. Infertility is still a huge part of our society, and 10–15 percent of couples will have difficulties achieving a pregnancy.[1] If you fall under this percentage, how will you react to your predicament? Will you become jealous and bitter like Rachel? Will you strike a deal like Hannah? Will you give up? Will you be like Isaac and fervently pray—and then watch to see how God uses your infertility to bless others and make all things good?

—

Dear God,

Thank you for choosing me to be part of this unique class of infertile women. You knew I was strong enough to handle this situation. I am anxious and excited to see what is in store for my life. Please be near me and help me center my thoughts on you. Amen.

WHAT DO YOU THINK?

What biblical character describes you and your infertility?

How do you see God using your infertility to help others?

YOU ARE PERFECT

I praise you because I am fearfully and wonderfully made;
your works are wonderful, I know that full well.
—Psalm 139:14

I recently attended a seminar on marital intimacy, which shared that the number one issue between a husband and a wife is the woman's insecurities regarding her body. "If only my stomach were flatter." "If only my backside were smaller." "If only my arms were more toned." "If only my nose were less pointy." "If only I had more eggs." "If only both sets of fallopian tubes worked." "If only I ovulated."

Insecurities arise, in part, because of comparisons with other people, jealousy of others, and the way society thinks a woman should be. The speaker challenged the audience to look into a mirror and thank God for every part of her own body, starting from the top of the head down to the tips of the toes.

We are made in the image of God. In God's very own image. Wow! Have you ever thought of that?

> So God created mankind in his own image, in the
> image of God he created them; male and female
> he created them. (Genesis 1:27)

God knows everything about our bodies. He knows how it works and even how many hairs are on our heads! We may feel like our bodies are broken or need a tune-up, but God sees us as his masterpieces. Look into a mirror and praise him today for the blessing of you.

—

Dear God,

Thank you for creating me in your perfect image. I praise you for every small detail. Help me not to compare myself to others or listen to what the world says. Help me be grateful for the body you have chosen for me. Amen.

WHAT DO YOU THINK?

What insecurities do you have about yourself?

How did you feel after looking in a mirror and thanking God for each part of you?

THE FAMILY UNIT

God saw all that he had made, and it was very good. And
there was evening, and there was morning—the sixth day.
—Genesis 1:31

The very first married couple ever recorded is Adam and Eve.
God created Eve so that Adam would not be alone and so that
his life would be complete. Once God created both Adam and
Eve, he "saw all that he had made and it was very good" (Genesis
1:31), and then he rested.

God had already created light and darkness, the waters, the
land, the animals, and humankind. Notice that God did not
create children, but he states that everything he created was
not just good, but very good. God knew that children were not
necessary to complete a man and a woman. The husband needs
the wife, and the wife needs the husband, but together they do not
need children. Together the husband-and-wife unit is all that is
necessary to form a family—to be a family. Having children does
not make you a family. Children enlarge an already established
family.

"When are you going to start a family?" It is a common
question people ask childless couples one year into the marriage.
Guess what? You already have started your family. You began
that family on the day you took your marriage vows. You and
your husband are a family. A family does not mean more than

two people. A family is two people who love each other, and that is very good!

—

Dear Lord,

Thank you for families. Help me focus on our love for each other and our commitment to each other through good times and through bad times. Amen.

WHAT DO YOU THINK?

*H*ow long have you been married?

*H*as someone asked when you were going to have a child? If so, how did you respond?

*W*hat is your favorite thing about your spouse?

Where Is the Intimacy?

But at the beginning of creation God made them male
and female. For this reason a man will leave his father and
mother and be united to his wife, and the two will become
one flesh. So they are no longer two, but one flesh.
—Mark 10:6–8

"Honey, come home from work now! I'm ovulating!" Sound
familiar? Month after month, year after year of trying to
conceive—and I was still not pregnant. Infertility was starting
to put a strain on our marriage. The "trying" part was not
fun anymore. Sex was neither exciting nor romantic. Sex was
becoming a chore—something we had to do at a specific time.
The only thing I focused on was making that baby. What could
I do to increase my odds of having a baby? Have we had enough
sex this month? Would this time finally work?

Our attitude toward sex put our marriage on the brink of
destruction. I was disappointed because I was not able to get
pregnant. My husband was upset because he could not provide
for me the one thing I so desperately desired. Our marriage was
suffering. There was no more hand-holding, goodbye kisses, or
warm embraces. Sex was merely an act—something we had to do
if we wanted to have children.

> Be completely humble and gentle; be patient, bearing with one another in love. Make every effort to keep the unity of the Spirit through the bond of peace. (Ephesians 4:2–3)

We did not want to give up on us. We did not want to give up on having a child either. We chose to fight for our marriage.

Marriage is hard. Infertility in marriage makes it even harder. It takes hard work, determination, perseverance, and patience, but God promises to see us through all things. He will be that strand of rope holding our marriage together.

> A cord of three strands is not quickly broken. (Ecclesiastes 4:12)

———

Dear Father,

Thank you for loving me. Create the intimacy in my marriage to make it how you designed it to be. Assure me that you have everything worked out in my marriage and my life journey. Amen.

What Do You Think?

What is your attitude toward sex and infertility?

How can you bring intimacy back into your relationship?

Why Does He Not Understand?

But to Hannah he gave a double portion because he
loved her, and the Lord had closed her womb.
—1 Samuel 1:5

My husband and I married in our late twenties. When we started
"trying" to conceive, it did not happen. Doctors told us that we
had less than a 1 percent chance of conceiving on our own. My
husband wanted to wait before jumping into fertility treatments.
It pained me. I wanted a baby and could feel my biological clock
ticking. Everywhere I turned, there was a baby—at the grocery
store, at church, and even at my exercise class. I was sad. I was
depressed. My husband did not understand. He did not realize
how much I desired a baby.

Wanting a baby is a natural feeling. God made women to
sincerely desire children. He made men to be protectors and
providers of their families. My husband was providing for me,
and he could not fathom why I was not happy. As men typically
do, he tried to fix the problem. He bought gifts for me and
took me on extravagant trips. He thought doing things for me
would make me feel satisfied, but I was not satisfied. I still
wanted a baby.

Husbands were much the same way in biblical times. In 1
Samuel, Hannah was married to Elkanah. For ten years, Hannah

and Elkanah tried to have a baby. As was the custom, after ten years with no children, a husband could take another wife to produce offspring. Elkanah married his second wife, and she produced numerous children for him. Elkanah was satisfied because his ancestry line would continue, but Hannah was still grieving. She desperately wanted a child of her own.

Every year, during a sacrificial time, Elkanah would give Hannah a double portion (more than his other wife). He displayed his great love for her, but it did not help Hannah's despair.

> Her husband Elkanah would say to her, "Hannah, why are you weeping? Why don't you eat? Why are you downhearted? Don't I mean more to you than ten sons?" (1 Samuel 1:8).

I wish I could grab Elkanah by the shoulders and give him a piece of my mind! "Come on, Elkanah. Do you not get it? Your wife is hurting—and you took another wife who is constantly tormenting and provoking her." Hannah must have heard the babies crying and seen her husband playing with the children and teaching them his craft. No extravagant gift or double portion would do. She wanted to hold her own baby.

One thing we can learn from this example is that we should not suffer alone. Hannah never confided in her husband. She was quiet and kept her pain to herself. God provides us with husbands to support us and guide us. God made husbands with the desire to protect us from our pain and suffering, but how can they do that if we do not talk to them about our feelings? God does not want us to bear this pain alone. He created the husband-and-wife unit to meet our needs of companionship and to model the relationship between God and his people. How can a marriage grow if we cannot share our deepest feelings with our best friend, our lover? We need to confide in our husbands, share our struggles with them, and pray together. Do not suffer from infertility alone. Talk with your man today!

—

Dear God,

Thank you for my husband. Help me be willing to share my pain and suffering with him. Guide our conversation. Help me with my frustration if he does not "get it" right away. Give me the words that he will understand. Thank you for providing this companionship. Amen.

WHAT DO YOU THINK?

*H*ow can you start sharing your needs with your husband?

*W*hat makes your relationship with your husband unique?

*D*oes your husband desire children?

I LOVE YOU. PLEASE
FORGIVE ME

In your anger do not sin. Do not let the sun
go down while you are still angry.
—Ephesians 4:26

"I love you. Please forgive me." Our marriage counselor told us certain phrases would be vital for a happy marriage. He was right. All marriages take hard work—and lots of it. Infertility made marriage even harder. Out of infertility grew seeds of bitterness and resentment.

I resented my husband because he did not want a baby immediately. I resented my husband because he wanted to pay off our debt before starting fertility treatments. I resented my husband because he was the reason for our infertility. Resentment was destroying our marriage, and my husband had no idea about my inner struggle. I was so wrapped up in my desire to get pregnant that I stopped communicating with him.

After months of therapy, I began to realize that resentment was hurting me more than my husband.

> Each one should test their own actions. Then they can take pride in themselves alone, without comparing themselves to someone else, for each one should carry their own load. (Galatians 6:4–5)

Once my heart softened, I began to see that my husband had the same desires, wants, and needs that I had.

Is there anything that is currently causing you resentment? If resentful thoughts have a grasp on us, we must let them go. We must release them and begin to take responsibility for—and control of—our actions. We must humble ourselves and change our hearts and attitudes.

> Whoever would foster love covers over an offense, but whoever repeats the matter separates close friends. (Proverbs 17:9)

"I love you. Please forgive me." Healing words can overcome resentful wounds.

—

Dear Lord,

Admitting that I am harboring resentful feelings is hard. Help me forgive so that bitterness does not harden my heart. Help me communicate and listen so I can walk in my marriage with the peace and understanding that comes from you. Amen.

WHAT DO YOU THINK?

*H*ow has infertility affected your marriage?

*W*hat are some of your unresolved resentments? How can you break free?

TICK TOCK

GIVE IT TO GOD—HE'S UP ALL NIGHT ANYWAY

Do not be anxious about anything, but in
every situation, by prayer and petition, with
thanksgiving, present your requests to God.
—Philippians 4:6

Scientifically speaking, there is a biological clock. It is easier to become pregnant and have a child in your twenties and thirties. The world would have you believe that a successful parent will fall somewhere in that age range. Anything older than that, and the critics will shame you. You will die and leave your child all alone, you will not be able to participate in activities with your child, or you will fail to understand your child.

Today, becoming a parent at a later age is possible through fertility treatments, surrogacy, and adoption. According to the Pew Research Center, first-time mothers are more likely to be thirty-five years old or older than two decades ago. In the past twenty years, the number of women having children in their mid-forties and beyond has tripled.[2]

"Age brings with it emotional stability, psychological strength, and financial security," says Pasquale Patrizio, MD, a professor with the department of obstetrics and gynecology at Yale School of Medicine and director of the Yale Fertility Center.[3]

In the Bible, Abraham and Sarah were well into their nineties when their son Isaac was born. Apparently, God does not view age as a factor for being a good parent. Why should we let age bother us?

> Therefore do not worry about tomorrow, for tomorrow will worry about itself. Each day has enough trouble of its own. (Matthew 6:34)

Let God handle the age critics. Today's trouble is enough for today. Trust that God knows best—and that miracles can happen through him.

⸺

Dear God,

It is so hard to stop worrying. Help me step out in faith and give you my anxious thoughts and desires. Help me keep my focus on you and not on the world. I know you have my future all worked out, and I am so grateful for that. Amen.

WHAT DO YOU THINK?

*W*hat causes you to worry?

*I*s your age causing you anxiety when it comes to bearing children?

What's Age Got to Do with It?

"Where is your wife Sarah?" they asked him. "There, in the tent," he said. Then one of them said, "I will surely return to you about this time next year, and Sarah your wife will have a son." Now Sarah was listening at the entrance to the tent, which was behind him. Abraham and Sarah were already very old, and Sarah was past the age of childbearing. So Sarah laughed to herself as she thought, "After I am worn out and my lord is old, will I now have this pleasure?" Then the Lord said to Abraham, "Why did Sarah laugh and say, 'Will I really have a child, now that I am old?' Is anything too hard for the Lord? I will return to you at the appointed time next year, and Sarah will have a son."
—Genesis 18:9–14

I married my husband in my late twenties and already had the mind-set that I had to "hurry" to get pregnant. I felt my biological clock ticking, mostly in part because I compared my life to my parents' lives. My mom was twenty-one years old when she was married and had her oldest child, me, at the age of twenty-five. In fact, she had all four of her kids by the time she turned thirty-one. I was twenty-eight, and I was just getting married. How was I going to bear all my children by the time I turned thirty-one? I put so much pressure on my marriage and myself. I was anxious, worried, and rushed. I just had to keep up.

If age does not concern God when it comes to parenting a child, why does the world make such a big deal about it? In the Bible, we read about ninety-year-old Sarah, Abraham's wife, giving birth to Isaac. We also learn about fourteen-year-old Mary giving birth to Jesus, God's son. God does not have a timetable.

> But do not forget this one thing, dear friends:
> With the Lord a day is like a thousand years, and
> a thousand years are like a day. (2 Peter 3:8)

No matter the age, all parents have one thing in common: the responsibility of caring for and loving another human being. God matches parents and children together perfectly. He does not make mistakes. A love between a parent and a child does not have a timetable. Love is merely that: love.

> Love is patient, love is kind. It does not envy,
> it does not boast, it is not proud. It does not
> dishonor others, it is not self-seeking, it is not
> easily angered, it keeps no record of wrongs. Love
> does not delight in evil but rejoices with the truth.
> It always protects, always trusts, always hopes,
> always perseveres. Love never fails. (1 Corinthians
> 13:4–8)

———

Dear God,

Help me remember that love is the only thing that matters. Turn my eyes toward you. Thank you for loving me so much. Amen.

WHAT DO YOU THINK?

What unnecessary timetable have you put on yourself and your situation?

How have you let society sway your thoughts?

THE HEART'S DAGGER

The Lord is close to the brokenhearted and
saves those who are crushed in spirit.
—Psalm 34:18

For my thirtieth birthday, my husband surprised me with a trip
to Las Vegas. He loves to play cards, I love the pool, and we both
enjoy the nightlife. Hours into this trip, I received news that
a good friend of mine was pregnant—another friend, another
pregnancy announcement, and another heartbreaking moment
acknowledging that I had yet to become a mother. And that was
not the first time. Every time, the news was harder and harder
to bear.

We live our lives trying to heal our wounds and pain all by
ourselves. We do so by keeping busy, stuffing our feelings, or even
turning to destructive behaviors. These measures are temporary
fixes to soothe the pain for a short while, but they can never truly
satisfy us.

God is closer than ever during these times of broken hearts.
When life hurts us the most, we need to look to the cross, where
Jesus also experienced pain and suffering. The power of the cross
is where healing truly begins.

Are you in a valley? Has your seed of bitterness taken root
and started to grow? We must turn our eyes toward Jesus. He is

the healer of broken hearts, and he wants to mend ours. He is the permanent fix to our crushed spirits.

> And we know that in all things God works for the good of those who love him, who have been called according to his purpose. (Romans 8:28)

This time is tough. It is very difficult to hear about fertility successes, pregnancy announcements, and babies being born. God knows our pain and suffering. He understands it better than anyone. He asks us to turn our eyes to him. He will take care of the rest.

~

Dear Jesus,

Thank you for bearing my pain and suffering on the cross. Please heal my broken heart and crushed spirit. Amen.

WHAT DO YOU THINK?

What emotions are you ignoring?

What behaviors are temporary fixes in your life?

WHERE DID THEY GO?

And the scripture was fulfilled that says, "Abraham
believed God, and it was credited to him as
righteousness," and he was called God's friend.
—James 2:23

Infertility consumed me. It was hard to be around people who
had children. It was even more difficult to see friends who were
pregnant. Reading a pregnancy announcement on social media
would put me into a tailspin. To top it all off, I did not want my
friends to know I was struggling with infertility issues. So, I
stopped reaching out altogether. I stopped being a friend.

Losing friends and close relationships is tough. It hurts, but
God has promised to be our friend. God created us in his image
so that we could have a personal relationship with him, a heart-
to-heart connection. God wants us to enter that secret place
of worship and friendship. He has promised never to leave us
nor forsake us. He will shout with heavenly songs in our joyful
moments and weep with us during our times of heartbreak and
despair. God can be our best friend.

What a friend we have in Jesus. All our sins and
griefs to bear! What a privilege to carry Everything
to God in prayer! Oh what peace we often forfeit;
Oh what needless pain we bear All because we do

not carry everything to God in prayer! Have we trials and temptations? Is there trouble anywhere? We should never be discouraged Take it to the Lord in prayer. Can we find a friend so faithful, Who will all our sorrows share? Jesus knows our every weakness Take it to the Lord in prayer. Are we weak and heavy-laden, Cumbered with a load of care? Precious Savior, still our refuge Take it to the Lord in prayer. Do your friends despise, forsake you? Take it to the Lord in prayer. In his arms he'll take and shield you; You wilt find a solace there.[4]

—

Dear God,

Thank you for being my friend. Help me remember that you are always there, waiting for me to come to you and start talking. I need you, God, more than ever. Amen.

What Do You Think?

Have you lost friends due to your infertility?

How have you coped with the loss of a friendship?

Keeping Up with the Joneses

Be content with what you have.
—Hebrews 13:5

Do you try to keep up with the Joneses? I am the first to admit that I fall into this trap. Ignoring the world is hard. It is difficult to stand firm and be satisfied with what God has already provided. God's Word tells us not to covet our neighbor's things. In fact, he knew the desire would be so hard that he listed it as one of his Ten Commandments. It is hard to keep this commandment when our desire is so strong. It becomes nearly impossible when a baby becomes the coveted item.

I struggled with this commandment. I wanted to feel a pregnant kick. I wanted to see two lines on a home pregnancy test. I wanted to make a pregnancy announcement. I wanted what she had. I wanted my pregnant friend's life.

"A heart at peace gives life to the body, but envy rots the bones" (Proverbs 14:30). Coveting brings bitterness, and bitterness brings jealousy. Jealously can create blinders to where we cannot see anything else. With envy, we can only see what is in front of us. We see what we do not have at that precise moment. In the midst of my infertility, I was so obsessed with what I did not have that I could not see the good. I could not see the other blessings that God was giving me. My vision was out of focus and blurry.

"Come near to God and he will come near to you" (James 4:8).

By drawing closer to God, my blinders came off. I was able to see more clearly. I began to appreciate the things I did have. I started to accept my infertility. By accepting this hardship, my soul began to heal. God was near me, and he had a reason for my infertility.

When things start looking cloudy again, I turn my thoughts to God and reach out to him. I put my focus and desires on Jesus. God has a plan for your infertility situation too. Take your blinders off and let him be the focus of your attention.

⁓

Dear God,

Help me remove the bitterness and jealousy that has consumed me. Help me focus on you and your purpose for my life. I have a road map that fits with what you want for me. Help clear my vision so that I can move forward with purpose and determination. Amen.

What Do You Think?

*W*hat have you coveted?

*H*ow can you remove jealousy from your life?

GOD GETS IT

The Lord himself goes before you and will be
with you; he will never leave you nor forsake you.
Do not be afraid; do not be discouraged.
—Deuteronomy 31:8

"Keeping trying—it will happen." "Relax." "Take a vacation—
and you'll come back pregnant." Sound familiar? These simple
words and phrases brought light to my infertility. There were
actual issues with my body and my husband's body that were
making it nearly impossible to create a baby. I did not want to hear
positive affirmations. I wanted realistic conversations. I wanted
real-life examples of successful fertility treatments. I was alone
in my struggle. I was alone in my heartbreak. I was alone in my
suffering. Nobody got it.

God gets it. Jesus lived on earth in human form, and because
of this, we know that he fully understands our struggles and
weaknesses. Jesus struggled with his emotions alone in the Garden
of Gethsemane. Jesus's heart broke when the people rejected him.
Jesus endured the pain and suffering of the cross. Jesus prayed
to his Father when he was in need, when he desired something.
He understands what we are going through. He knows when we
are strong, and he also knows when we need someone to carry us
through troubled times. Rest assured that he knows exactly what

we are experiencing. He has promised never to leave us nor forsake us. God gets us!

> One night I dreamed a dream. As I was walking along the beach with my Lord, across the dark sky flashed scenes from my life. For each scene, I noticed two sets of footprints in the sand, one belonging to me and one to my Lord. After the last scene of my life flashed before me, I looked back at the footprints in the sand. I noticed that at many times along the path of my life, especially at the very lowest and saddest times, there was only one set of footprints. This really troubled me, so I asked the Lord about it. "Lord, you said once I decided to follow You, You'd walk with me all the way. But I noticed that during the saddest and most troublesome times of my life, there was only one set of footprints. I don't understand why, when I needed you the most, you would leave me." He whispered, "My precious child, I love you and will never leave you never, ever, during your trials and testing. When you saw only one set of footprints, it was then that I carried you."[5]

We must reach out to God when we are grieving, anxious, or in despair. He will guide us and carry us until we can walk alongside him again.

Dear Lord,

Please be with me when I struggle with things I cannot control, when people say things that are hurtful, and when I feel like I cannot take any more bad news. Help me remember that you get it, that you understand my struggles, and that you will carry me along this path that I am on. In you alone, I will put my trust. Amen.

WHAT DO YOU THINK?

What phrases have brought light to your infertility?

What will help you feel less alone in your infertility battle?

PLEASE, PRETTY PLEASE!

> The woman came and knelt before him.
> "Lord, help me!" she said.
> —Matthew 15:25

In the book of Matthew, there is a woman who has a demonically possessed daughter. The woman followed Jesus on his vacation to plead and beg for his help. She asked him over and over again to save her daughter from the daily torment of the spiritual forces within her.

At first, Jesus ignored the woman. He told her that he only helps those of Israel. She was not of that genetic line. He then compared her to a dog, begging its owner for a scrap of food. Imagine our reaction to Jesus if he said that to us. Would you continue to ask—or would you accept your daughter's fate and walk away?

This woman continued to beg for mercy. She did not get angry. She did not walk away. She did not get discouraged. She simply kept asking and pleading with Jesus. She believed that Jesus could and would help heal her daughter. Jesus commended this woman on her steadfast faith, and in the end, he granted her request. Jesus healed her daughter.

Jesus never told the woman no. She waited. During her waiting period, she pleaded. She persisted. She never gave up. She continued onward with her pleas.

Do you wait for an answer—or are you impatient and want to give up? Jesus wants to say yes to our requests even when it appears he does not. Sometimes, he wants us to wait so that our faith and trust in him will grow. He wants us to share our steadfast faith with others. God will hear us and answer our prayers in his perfect time.

Dear God,

Thank you for your miraculous healings. Thank you for listening and hearing my prayers. Help me learn to wait and never give up. Amen.

WHAT DO YOU THINK?

What are you asking of God?

How can you be more persistent in your faith?

THE WAITING GAME

Wait for the Lord; be strong and take
heart and wait for the Lord.
—Psalm 27:14

I am a very punctual person and with that comes a lot of waiting.
I hate waiting. Despise it. I always have. It feels like I have been
waiting for something or someone all my life. So, imagine my
anxiety while waiting every month to see if I was pregnant. It
was brutal.

Waiting is not easy. It never is when the anticipation is so
great. You may be waiting for an adoption to go through. You may
be in the two-week wait window after a fertility treatment. You
may be waiting nine months to finally meet your baby.

Waiting on God is not easy either. It often seems that he is
not answering our prayers.

> I say to myself, "The Lord is my portion; therefore
> I will wait for him." The Lord is good to those
> whose hope is in him, to the one who seeks him;
> it is good to wait quietly for the salvation of the
> Lord. (Lamentations 3:24–26)

Patience is one of the eight attributes in God's fruit of the
spirit. God instructs us to be patient as we grow in our Christian

walk. Many times, God will use our waiting periods to refresh us, to renew us, and to teach us. What is God trying to show you through your waiting period? Stay strong. It will be worth the wait!

———

Dear God,

Help me wait on you and your timing. I know your plan is perfect. Help me be more patient and glorify you in all things. Amen.

What Do You Think?

What are you waiting for?

Why do you think God is making you wait?

PURIFIED IN THE WAITING

But as for me, I watch in hope for the Lord, I wait
for God my Savior; my God will hear from me.
—Micah 7:7

We spend a lot of time waiting. We wait for something to happen, wait on people, and even wait on God. How do you handle your waiting time? Do you grow anxious and weary? Do you sit around and twiddle your thumbs? Do you pray nonstop or page through the Bible, looking for clues? The Bible tells us to wait on the Lord. "Wait for the Lord; be strong and take heart and wait for the Lord" (Psalm 27:14). The Bible also provides many examples of biblical characters waiting on God. Their journeys and their experiences can help us as we wait.

Daniel prayed and fasted for twenty-one days as he waited on the Lord. As Paul was waiting in prison, he began to pray, write, and journal. Many of his works are found in the Bible today. Hannah prayed for nineteen years while she waited for a baby. During those nineteen years, she battled tension and torment from her sister-wife Peninnah. Unlike Rachel, Jacob's wife, and Sarah, Abraham's wife, who also battled infertility, Hannah did not use a maidservant to conceive a child. Hannah kept her suffering to herself. She was quiet and would cry out to God. She did not fight back. She did not seek revenge. She simply took her request to God. She never abandoned her goal of becoming a mother. She continued to persevere in hope and prayer.

Hannah's prayer changed during her nineteen years. She now prayed that if God granted her a son, she would give that child back to him. She was willing to give up her desire of raising her child. She was willing to sacrifice her blessing to God. God gave her a son, Samuel. "I prayed for this child, and the Lord granted me what I asked of him" (1 Samuel 1:27). Hannah honored her vow by giving Samuel back to God. God honored her sacrifice by blessing her with three more sons and two daughters.

God wants us to give him our entire selves—whether it is giving up food for twenty-one days, spilling our most profound thoughts and concerns on paper, or even willingly sacrificing something we so desperately desire—but God will not be able to do anything while we wait if we do not take the first step. We must seek him out. We must start the conversation. We must pray. God promises that he will hear us as we wait. Keep hoping, keep praying, and keep persevering.

—

Dear God,

Help me as I wait. Guide my prayer life, my thoughts, and my actions as I wait. I give you all the honor and glory. Amen.

WHAT DO YOU THINK?

*W*hat are you doing as you wait on the Lord? Have you fasted? Studied? Made a vow?

*A*s you wait on God, have your prayers changed? If so, how?

*H*ow can you encourage others as they wait on God?

I THINK WAY TOO MUCH!

Come to me, all you who are weary and burdened, and I will
give you rest. Take my yoke upon you and learn from me,
for I am gentle and humble in heart, and you will find rest
for your souls. For my yoke is easy and my burden is light.
—Matthew 11:28–30

Month after month, year after year, cycle after cycle, and I was still
not pregnant. My hopes and dreams of becoming a mother were
slowly fading away. I was losing faith. I began to imagine worst-
case scenarios to protect myself from another negative pregnancy
test. Negativity consumed my thoughts. God's Word tells us that
our thoughts dictate who we become. "As water reflects the face,
so one's life reflects the heart" (Proverbs 27:19). Was my fear of
being hurt and feeling let down, again and again, dictating who
I was becoming?

In the devotional *Jesus Calling*, the author informs us that
"rehashing our troubles has us experience the negative result over
and over again."[6] God's intent is not for that to happen. God is
good. He does not want our attitudes to be negative. He does not
want us to suffer. Why do we put our sufferings on a pedestal?
Why do we make our negativity larger than life?

If something has taken place that is not what we hoped for,
such as a negative pregnancy test, a miscarriage, a failed adoption,
or an unsuccessful fertility treatment, God wants us to go through

that circumstance one time—in that one moment. We should not be reliving it over and over again. It should not consume us. Rehashing the situation will not result in a different outcome. We cannot change the past. We cannot change what occurred. God tells us to come to him and give him our burdens, our anxious thoughts, and our worries. He will strengthen us and bring us through the valleys. Stop thinking so much about the past—or even future outcomes—and focus on the present. Let God take care of the rest.

~

Dear God,

Help me stop worrying about the future. Help me put my trust in you. I know that you work everything for your good. Thank you for loving me. Amen.

WHAT DO YOU THINK?

*W*hat do your thoughts say about you?

*W*hat are you reliving time and time again? How can you move forward?

A "Doubting Thomas" Way of Life

Then Jesus told him, "Because you have seen
me, you have believed; blessed are those who
have not yet seen and yet have believed."
—John 20:29

I am a glass-half-empty person. My attitude leans more toward negativity and doubt. After months of reading negative home pregnancy tests, my approach toward conceiving became pessimistic. I felt defeated. Pregnancy was doubtful. I was losing hope.

Doubt can sneak through the cracks and suffocate our faith. As soon as circumstances do not go our way, we start doubting God and his plan for our life. We began asking God questions such as, "Are you there, God?" "Are you listening?" "Do you even care what I am going through?" We become frustrated, disappointed, and unsure of where life is taking us. The enemy wants us to dwell on our doubt. He wants us to feel like God is not listening to our prayers.

The disciple Thomas was filled with grief and doubt after the death of his Lord, Jesus Christ. John tells the story of the resurrected Jesus appearing to his disciples to comfort them and proclaim victory over death. Only one disciple was missing. Thomas was not present during Jesus's visit. Thomas doubted the disciples' story. He needed to see proof. Jesus knew Thomas's weakness and appeared to him. Jesus gave him the proof of his scarred hands and feet. Only then did Thomas believe. Only then did Thomas's doubt go away.

Are you waiting for a Thomas moment? Jesus does not tell us that he will comfort our doubts by giving us what we want—or what we think we need. We may not receive a colossal miraculous circumstance. Unlike Thomas, however, Jesus has given us his Holy Spirit to indwell in us and strengthen our faith.

Christ is always around us. He is always inviting us to touch him and see him. Look at the birds of the air, the flowers' first buds in spring, or the sun setting over the mountains. He knows our weakness of doubt. Praying, reading the Bible, and surrounding ourselves with encouraging Christian fellowship can dissipate any negative feelings we might have. Don't let a "doubting Thomas" attitude affect your faith and your walk with Christ. Our glass can become half full by centering our thoughts on what God has for our lives and our futures.

~

Dear God,

Help strengthen my faith when doubt starts to creep in. Create positive attitudes in us. Keep my eyes focused on you and your wants for my life. Amen.

What Do You Think?

*A*re you a positive or a negative person?

*W*hat are ways that you can curb your doubt?

ANOTHER CELEBRATION

Come, let us sing for joy to the Lord: let us
shout aloud to the Rock of our salvation.
—Psalm 95:1

I did not notice my first childless Mother's Day. The second one was a bit harder. By the time the third one hit, I was miserable. It pained me to see the advertisements celebrating motherhood. Church was difficult as mothers received special recognition. Social media was unbearable. Mother's Day was a reminder of something I longed for but did not have. It was a day where I felt sorry for myself and felt the pains of jealousy. I wanted a celebration. I wanted to surround myself with my own children.

Mother's Day is not the only holiday I dreaded. Christmas and Halloween were just as hard. I desperately wanted to be part of the "hoopla." I wanted to post my cute pictures on social media for the world to see. I wanted to parade my children through the neighborhood to ask for candy. I wanted to stuff my child's Christmas stocking. All holidays were weighing on my heart.

RESOLVE, the National Infertility Association, outlines six ways to cope with infertility during a holiday.

- Take a proactive stance. Think ahead about the day and plan a strategy. Do not wait until the holiday is upon you to make plans.
- Focus on your parents, grandparents, or another special parental figure. Make this a special time for them. If pleasant for you, go enjoy a family gathering.
- Recognize potential painful situations. Restaurants and churches, for example, may be a source of discomfort. They may ask if you are a mother or a father to give you a complimentary item. Be prepared for this question so it does not come as a surprise.
- Consider joining a support group or reaching out to a friend. A support group will help you feel less isolated, empower you with knowledge, and validate your emotional response to the life crisis of infertility.
- Speak to your pastor. Before a religious service, talk with your clergyperson and educate him or her about the experience of infertility. Perhaps he or she would be willing to say a prayer or offer words of support for those struggling with this crisis.
- Plan an enjoyable day together. It is important to work as a couple during these difficult days. Consider tuning out the holiday emphasis entirely and make it an opportunity for a fun day together.[7]

Ecclesiastes says that there is a time for everything, "a time to weep and a time to laugh, a time to mourn and a time to dance" (Ecclesiastes 3:4). In your current situation, it might not be a time of celebration. You may be mourning a miscarriage or longing for a child's embrace. It is okay to feel this way. We must turn our pain and heartache toward God. He will lift us up and give us the strength we need.

But those who hope in the Lord will renew their strength. They will soar on wings like eagles; they will run and not grow weary, they will walk and not be faint. (Isaiah 40:31)

~

Dear God,

Holidays can be difficult. Help me turn my thoughts and attention toward you. Give me hope for the future and confidence knowing you have everything worked out for my life. Amen.

WHAT DO YOU THINK?

How can you ease your infertility pain during a holiday?

Have you asked your spouse how he feels during a holiday? Share your ideas and thoughts to make it easier for the both of you.

TRAPPED IN THE TOMB

Trembling and bewildered, the women went
out and fled from the tomb. They said nothing
to anyone, because they were afraid.
—Mark 16:8

Every month was the same. I would get my hopes up that it was going to be the month! This would be the month that I was going to be pregnant. Instead, month after month, I was filled with disappointment and grief. I experienced another negative pregnancy test and another failed attempt. Sorrow and despair consumed me. I felt trapped in a world of grief—in a land between what could have been and what I could not see.

People deal with pain and grief in three different ways:

1. Choosing to downplay the pain by avoiding the pain altogether.
2. Denying the pain by escaping it. These people become super busy to numb the pain.
3. Drowning in pain. We start becoming what has happened to us. The pain is all-consuming.

How was I dealing with my unfortunate fate every month? God wants to lead us through this unknown land to triumph. He tells us to serve him in 100 percent of what we have now—not what we had in the past and not what will be in the future but right now! He tells us to press into the pain entirely. He will be waiting on the other side with open arms. He also says to keep waiting and persevere.

Luke tells us that our waiting should not be wishful waiting, where instant results happen, and the results are what we want. Instead, we should be actively waiting, where we are persisting in hope.

> Be dressed ready for service and keep your lamps burning, like servants waiting for their master to return from a wedding banquet, so that when he comes and knocks they can immediately open the door for him. (Luke 12:35–36)

Jesus rose from the grave. He triumphed over the tomb. He did not lay to rest in it forever. In the same way, he does not want us to rest inside our tomb of pain, grief, and despair. The best is yet to come!

———

Dear God,

Help me deal head-on with my pain. The enemy keeps lying to me that this is where you want me to be, but I know that is not the case. I know you want to lead me through this pain to triumph. Help me on my path to victory through you. Amen.

WHAT DO YOU THINK?

*H*ow do you deal with pain and disappointment?

*H*ow can you actively wait?

CHOICES

WHOSE TEAM ARE YOU ON?

Do not be yoked together with unbelievers. For what
do righteousness and wickedness have in common?
Or what fellowship can light have with darkness?
—2 Corinthians 6:14

I was super excited for our first fertility appointment. We were finally taking steps for a baby. Our doctor had a soft demeanor that made us feel comfortable. He wanted us to have a baby just as much as we wanted to have a baby. He walked us through the steps of our reproductive issues and explained that in vitro fertilization (IVF) was our only option to achieve a pregnancy. As he was walking out of the room, he gave us paperwork to read about IVF.

The paperwork contained numerous questions about our faith and our beliefs. It asked, "When do you believe life begins?" and "What will you do with the extra embryos?" We were deeply concerned. What really was IVF? Doctors needed to retrieve as many eggs from my body as possible and fertilize them with my husband's sperm. Creating as many embryos as possible is what can make or break a successful IVF outcome. The more eggs that fertilize, the better the chances of a successful pregnancy and live birth. My husband and I believe that life begins at conception.

For you created my inmost being; you knit me together in my mother's womb. (Psalm 139:13)

Paul tells us in Corinthians not to team up with unbelievers because it might weaken our faith. This does not mean to separate ourselves from unbelievers. As Christians, we are to be strong witnesses, not wavering in our faith. In this instance, our faith and viewpoint on life needed to be stronger than IVF's most successful way. We were on God's team, and that team viewed embryos as lives—not pieces of conception and not something to discard after use.

After much prayer and pastoral guidance, we still felt God opening the door to IVF. However, the godly advice was specific. We could only create embryos that we were going to use. We had to overcome the pressure from doctors and the clinic staff to produce more. We had to accept the fact that IVF might not be successful. We would not compromise our beliefs.

God tells us that the fight might not be easy. There will be struggles along the way, but we must persevere.

I press on toward the goal to win the prize for which God has called me heavenward in Christ Jesus. (Philippians 3:14)

Dear God,

Thank you for showing me your way. Please help me hold true to your way and your path even when the world suggests a different course. I need your strength daily and pray for your peace. Amen.

What Do You Think?

How have you overcome the pressures of the world?

What or who can help you when you face difficult situations?

GOD KNOWS YOUR FUTURE

The Lord said to Satan, "Very well, then, he is
in your hands; but you must spare his life."
—Job 2:6

The Bible tells us a story about a man named Job. Job is devoted to God. Because of this devotion and trust, God has blessed Job with a family, wealth, and much happiness in life. In fact, the Bible states that he was the wealthiest man in the area.

God told Satan that he could take away all of Job's possessions, his children, and his health. When this happened, Job's wife and friends advised Job to curse God and turn away from him. Job's response to his hardship was simple, "Shall we accept good from God, and not trouble?" (Job 2:10).

Every day, we are battling a war between the spirit and the flesh. Every day, we have the choice to follow God or follow the world. God knows our exact situation. He knows when our lives seem difficult. He knows the decisions we face daily. God will not give us more than we can handle, but he might let us bend. God works for the good of those who love him. Our hardships and struggles might provide help for those who come after us. Our example of faithfully following God could turn someone to Christ.

Fight what the world has to offer or sees as normal. God is

on the offense. He will not give up or leave us alone. He will be with us as long as we stay close to him.

~

Dear God,

I am often filled with uncertainty and questions. Help me stay close to you. Guide my steps always. Amen.

WHAT DO YOU THINK?

What can you learn from Job?

Why did God allow Job to be tested?

How do you respond to hardships?

WHAT ARE YOU WEARING?

> Put on the full armor of God, so that you can
> take your stand against the devil's schemes.
> —Ephesians 6:11

Living for God takes hard work and determination. Christians are battling worldly pressures and fighting a spiritual war.

> For our struggle is not against flesh and blood,
> but against the rulers, against the authorities,
> against the powers of this dark world and against
> the spiritual forces of evil in the heavenly realms.
> (Ephesians 6:12)

Satan's evil angels are also known as demons. These dark forces are meant for harm and can influence our lives when we least expect it. Any area of life is susceptible to an attack. Demons can enter our lives when we receive bad news, when the outcome is disappointing, or when a tough decision is needed. Satan wants to rob us of our joy. He wants to destroy our hope. He desires bad results. By letting disappointment and impossibility consume us, we allow darkness and evil to take root. Once a root grows, it can turn into something ugly and unimaginable.

During the infertility journey, there are many times when there seems to be no hope. There is much disappointment and grief. God tells us not to despair—and to put our faith and our trust in him.

> Be always on the watch, and pray that you may be able to escape all that is about to happen, and that you may be able to stand before the Son of Man. (Luke 21:36)

God tells us in Ephesians that we need to protect ourselves from this spiritual war taking place in our lives.

> Stand firm then, with the belt of truth buckled around your waist, with the breastplate of righteousness in place, and with your feet fitted with the readiness that comes from the gospel of peace. In addition to all this, take up the shield of faith, with which you can extinguish all the flaming arrows of the evil one. Take the helmet of salvation and the sword of the Spirit, which is the word of God. (Ephesians 6:14–17)

We cannot take on demonic forces by ourselves. God will fight the battle for us.

> The Lord will fight for you; you need only to be still. (Exodus 14:14)

God can break the chains of depression, hopelessness, and fear of the unknown. He is the overcomer we so desperately need in our lives. We must fully surrender ourselves to him to live in his light of everlasting peace and hope. Be sure you are wearing the correct armor!

~

Dear Father,

Help me when there seems to be no hope. Protect me from the evil one. Guide my mind and my heart. I love you. Amen.

What Do You Think?

Name a time when Satan has robbed you of your joy. How have you overcome this?

What area of your life is not entirely given over to God? Is there a reason for this?

Choice Overflow

Finally, brothers and sisters, whatever is true, whatever
is noble, whatever is right, whatever is pure, whatever is
lovely, whatever is admirable—if anything is excellent
or praiseworthy—think about such things.
—Philippians 4:8

There are many fertility-treatment options. How do you know
which treatment is right for your family? The Bible is the
guidebook for making wise decisions.

Dale Robbins shares sixteen biblical scriptures and questions
we should be asking ourselves before making decisions.

> Before you make decisions, compare your desires
> to what the scriptures say, and ask yourself the
> following questions:

1. Would you be able to ask God to bless it? Would your
   decision be something that you can take before God
   with a good conscience and ask Him to bless? Or is it
   something that you know the Lord would not be enthused
   about. "The blessing of the Lord brings wealth, without
   painful toil for it" (Proverbs 10:22).
2. Can you thank God for it? Would your decision be
   something that you can openly express gratefulness

and thankfulness to God? Or would it be something that would seem inappropriate to thank him for? "And whatever you do, whether in word or deed, do all in the name of the Lord Jesus, giving thanks to God the Father through him" (Colossians 3:17).

3. Would it be to God's Glory? Would your decision be something that can bring Glory and honor to the Lord? "So whether you eat or drink or whatever you do, do all for the glory of God" (1 Corinthians 10:31).

4. Would it be of the world? Would your decision be an indulgence upon worldly, carnal appetites or lusts? "Do not love the world or anything in the world. If anyone loves the world, the love for the Father is not in them" (1 John 2:15).

5. Would it be a stumbling block to others? How would your decision affect the lives of others? Even if you don't feel it's wrong, could it offend or harm the sensitive faith of those who don't share your convictions? "Be careful, however, that the exercise of your rights does not become a stumbling block to the weak" (1 Corinthians 8:9).

6. Would it be a weight or hindrance? Would your decision be something that would drag down your Christian life or influence you toward disobedience? "Let us throw off everything that hinders and the sin that so easily entangles. And let us run with perseverance the race marked out for us" (Hebrews 12:1).

7. Would it please God or man? Whom do you hope to please by your decision? Will it bring pleasure to God, or will it appease self or man? "Whatever you do, work at it with all your heart, as working for the Lord, not for human masters" (Colossians 3:23).

8. How would the Devil react? Would your decision be considered a victory or a defeat by the Devil's forces? Would Hell celebrate your choice as a fulfillment of Satan's desires—or would the enemy be angry and

disturbed? "Be alert and of sober mind. Your enemy the devil prowls around like a roaring lion looking for someone to devour. Resist him, standing firm in the faith, because you know that the family of believers throughout the world is undergoing the same kind of sufferings" (1 Peter 5:8–9).

9. What would the consequences be? What kind of long-term ramifications would you have to face for your decision? Remember, God will forgive sin and poor judgment, but you may have to live with the results of your decision for the rest of your life. "Do not be deceived: God cannot be mocked. A man reaps what he sows" (Galatians 6:7).

10. Would it edify you? Would your decision or actions bring you closer to God or pull you farther away? Will it build you up in the Lord or will it weaken your confidence of the Lord's strength in your life? "'I have the right to do anything,' you say—but not everything is beneficial. 'I have the right to do anything'—but not everything is constructive" (1 Corinthians 10:23).

11. Would it serve the right master? Will your decision require you to yield to the demands of someone or something other than Christ? Will it cause you to compromise your submission and obedience to Jesus? "No one can serve two masters. Either you will hate the one and love the other, or you will be devoted to the one and despise the other" (Matthew 6:24).

12. Would God's indwelling presence agree with it? Would your decision bring peace to your inner man, or would it create discomfort or distress? Is your choice directed by the promptings and leadings of the Holy Spirit, or by the appetites of the flesh? "But when he, the Spirit of truth, comes, he will guide you into all the truth" (John 16:13).

13. Would you want to be doing this when Jesus returns? Would you want to be doing this when Christ comes

again? If Jesus appeared before you to inspect your decision or actions, would you be embarrassed or delighted? Would his presence make you comfortable or insecure? "So you also must be ready, because the Son of Man will come at an hour when you do not expect him" (Matthew 24:44).

14. Would it promote love? Would your decision or actions express love and harmony, or would it reflect retribution, jealousy or injury to your neighbor? "Let no debt remain outstanding, except the continuing debt to love one another, for whoever loves others has fulfilled the law" (Romans 13:8).

15. Have you sought the Lord about it? The Lord promises to give leadership and direction to our life. Consult him in prayer. Remember, God will never speak something to our heart that contradicts his written Word. "In all your ways submit to him, and he will make your paths straight" (Proverbs 3:6).

16. Have you sought godly counsel or advice? Ask the advice of those who live godly lives and have a track record of experience and wise decision-making. Avoid the counsel of those whose Christian life is questionable or who have experience of failure in making sound decisions. "For lack of guidance a nation falls, but victory is won through many advisers" (Proverbs 11:14).[8]

—

Dear God,

Please help me make the right decision. My desires are too much at times, and I need your guidance. Please give me peace. Help me be still and listen to your voice. Thank you for your direction in my life. Amen.

WHAT DO YOU THINK?

*D*o you pray about your decisions? Do you pray about all your choices?

*H*ow can you be sure your decision lines up with God's will?

God, Our Father

I prayed for this child, and the Lord has
granted me what I asked of him.
—1 Samuel 1:27

More than one hundred thousand children in the United States
are waiting to be adopted.[9] More than five hundred thousand
embryos are also waiting for a forever family.[10]

One of the first accounts of adoption mentioned in the New
Testament is the story of Jesus.

> But after he had considered this, an angel of the
> Lord appeared to him in a dream and said, "Joseph,
> son of David, do not be afraid to take Mary home
> as your wife, because what is conceived in her is
> from the Holy Spirit. She will give birth to a son,
> and you are to give him the name Jesus, because
> he will save his people from their sins." When
> Joseph woke up, he did what the angel of the Lord
> had commanded him and took Mary home as his
> wife. But he did not consummate their marriage
> until she gave birth to a son. And he gave him the
> name Jesus. (Matthew 1:20–21; 24–25)

A legal adoption with a judge and a court process did not take place, but the Jewish society accepted Jesus as Joseph's earthly son.

I imagine Joseph was worried about the thought of providing for a child. I imagine Joseph was concerned about what others might think. I imagine Joseph was afraid he would not be a good enough father for this child. Did it cross Joseph's mind if he would be able to love Jesus just as if he were his own?

Today, couples considering adoption have much to think about: domestic or international, boy or girl, baby, toddler, child, or an embryo, open adoption or a closed one. My husband and I considered infant adoption as well as embryo adoption. In fact, we put our names on an embryo adoption list, which was a long list.

Adoption is another type of fertility treatment with ups and downs. There are hopeless nights and heartbreak. There is pain. "Will someone choose us to parent their child?" "Will the birth mother give up her rights?" "Will the birth parents change their minds?" "Will the paperwork fall through?" "How long must we wait?"

God knows all about adoption. He has adopted us as his children. He knows the joy it feels to finally hold you in his arms. Our godly adoption has secured our citizenship in heaven. Praise God for that!

> He predestined us for adoption to sonship through
> Jesus Christ, in accordance with his pleasure and
> will. (Ephesians 1:5)

~

Dear God,

Thank you for adopting us and loving us. Please guide our steps and help us determine your will for our lives. Amen.

WHAT DO YOU THINK?

*H*ow do you feel about adoption?

*I*s God calling you and your spouse toward adoption?

TRUTH TELLER

But Sarah saw that the son whom Hagar the Egyptian had
borne to Abraham was mocking, and she said to Abraham,
"Get rid of that slave woman and her son for that woman's son
will never share in the inheritance with my son Isaac." The
matter distressed Abraham greatly because it concerned his son.
—Genesis 21:9–11

Many fertility treatments require a sperm donor or an egg donor.
Most biblical scholars and pastors disagree with this concept.
How much scientific advancement honors God? Does God desire
us to partake in all types of fertility treatment? Sperm and egg
donation tampers with the marriage unit. God designed marriage
to be a union between a man and a woman.

> That is why a man leaves his father and mother
> and is united to his wife, and they become one
> flesh. (Genesis 2:24)

The Bible shares a story regarding sperm donation. The
account comes from Genesis. God told Sarah and Abraham that
they would have a child. Because Sarah was old and believed
to be barren, she told Abraham to sleep with her maidservant,
Hagar. The child Hagar conceived would be adopted into their
family and raised as their own. Sarah and Abraham took matters

into their own hands. They did not trust that God would provide a baby. They did not believe that Sarah would indeed become pregnant.

Hagar conceived a child from Abraham's donated seed, and Ishmael was born. Ishmael became the father of the Muslim nation. This nation caused much unrest for the Jewish people, God's chosen. Even to this day, wars and battles are still taking place. Sarah grew jealous of Hagar and the son between Abraham and Hagar. I imagine the marriage unit between Abraham and Sarah became strained. I imagine jealousy and bitterness arose in their marriage. As the verse states above, Sarah asked Abraham to cast out Hagar and Ishmael. The plan of raising Ishmael went out the window once Sarah bore Isaac. Distrust in God caused much adversity in the world and in the marriage.

God did not condemn Sarah and Abraham. God still provided life. He allowed Sarah and Abraham to make an unwise decision. Sometimes unwise choices can have consequences we may not like. We have to learn to live with those decisions whether good or bad. God promises that he will be with us through it all. We need to trust God even when there seems to be no way. God can do all things!

—

Dear God,

Provide me with the wisdom to make decisions that are pleasing to you. Infertility has many treatment choices, and it is challenging to navigate a way through them. Guide my heart and mind to trust and follow you. Amen.

WHAT DO YOU THINK?

Do you think God desires us to use all types of fertility treatments?

Is there a time in your life where God told you something was going to happen, and instead of waiting, you took matters into your own hands? What was the outcome of doing so?

OUR MINDS

Therefore, holy brothers and sisters, who share in the
heavenly calling, fix your thoughts on Jesus, whom
we acknowledge as our apostle and high priest.
—Hebrews 3:1

Anything we want to know is right at our fingertips. With a
click of a button, we can search for a specific product, read the
latest news headlines, and get answers to our most sought-after
questions. We can research ailments and diseases. We can connect
with others going through similar circumstances.

During my infertility journey, I spent most of my free time
researching fertility treatments, reading successful pregnancy
outcomes, and trying to solve the aches and pains associated
with my treatment protocol. My mind was on overload with the
amount of stuff that is on the internet regarding infertility. What
was true? What was untrue?

When we overthink, we often focus on adverse outcomes or
problems that could arise. We keep circling our situation in hopes
of gaining control over it and our emotions. We lose so much
energy playing out a scenario over and over again that we lose
focus on the one thing that matters: Jesus Christ.

Finally, brothers and sisters, whatever is true,
whatever is noble, whatever is right, whatever is

pure, whatever is lovely, whatever is admirable—
if anything is excellent or praiseworthy—think
about such things. (Philippians 4:8)

Overthinking can cause unnecessary worry and anxiety. Worrying can cause many damaging impacts. Anxiety can impair our health, affect our relationships, and hinder our trust in God.

We must continually renew our minds and center our thoughts on God. God wants us to focus our attention on him. We can read the Bible, pray, take a walk, and observe nature. God is everywhere and even more accessible than technology. Only he can provide us with answers and peace.

～

Dear God,

Please help me focus on you. I love you, and I know you have everything under control. Amen.

What Do You Think?

What websites consume you?

How can you renew your mind?

Do You Trust God?

Trust in the Lord with all your heart and
lean not on your own understanding.
—Proverbs 3:5

I have a type A personality. I like order. I love plans. When the decision was made to pursue IVF, my husband and I planned to fertilize ten eggs. We planned to use all ten embryos if fertilization occurred positively. Yes, that means ten children!

On the day of my egg-retrieval surgery, the embryologist removed sixteen eggs from my body. Doctors fertilized our planned ten eggs. The other six eggs remained in the lab, untouched and unfertilized. Out of the ten fertilized eggs, only four were sustainable embryos and growing into life. I was in panic mode. I did not plan for this. I wanted more usable embryos. The surviving embryos needed to remain in a petri dish for two more days before transferring them back into my body. Would they survive two more days? I needed a plan, and I needed it fast.

Without consulting my husband or praying about it, I put my new plan into action. I told the embryologist to fertilize the remaining six eggs that were still in the lab. The embryologist advised against it, but without hesitation, I told him to move forward with the new plan. I needed that baby. The next morning, doctors called with bad news. The six eggs from the lab did not fertilize into life. In fact, doctors used the word "abnormal." Did I create life only to throw it away?

Two days later, we prepared for the embryo transfer. All four embryos were still alive. One was developing slowly, one was growing too fast, and two were growing precisely as they should be. Two were perfect embryos. Perfect. God's perfection at work. The transfer went smoothly, and six weeks later, we were expecting twins.

God's plan was perfect. God knew the result the entire time. Instead, I tried to push my agenda, which caused years of guilt and shame for compromising my beliefs. God had our situation under control. As the song says, "He's Got the Whole World in His Hands."[11]

—

Dear God,

It is so hard to be patient. I often find myself moving forward with my agenda without consulting you. Help me remember that you have already planned out every aspect of my life. Help me put my full trust in you. Amen.

WHAT DO YOU THINK?

Describe a time you made a quick decision and later regretted it?

What plans are you trying to push on God right now?

My Mistake

But while he was still a long way off, his father saw him and
was filled with compassion for him; he ran to his son, threw
his arms around him and kissed him. "For this son of mine
was dead and is alive again; he was lost and is found."
—Luke 15:20; 24

In the book of Luke, Jesus tells us a story about a father with
two sons. The younger son decides to take his inheritance and
leave his father's house. He spends all his money and ends up
living with the pigs. The younger son returns home with the
intent of begging for his father's forgiveness. Much to the younger
son's surprise, his father runs to him, takes him in his arms, and
celebrates his return with no strings attached. The father was
happy that his son was home.

I am that prodigal son. I strayed from my heavenly Father.
I made a mistake. My anxiety and greed initiated my mistake.
I tried to handle my problems when God had everything under
control. During our IVF procedure, doctors told us four embryos
had fertilized positively. Four embryos were living and sustaining
life. If those embryos implanted inside my body, four children
were in our future. I was not happy with four. I wanted more. I
wanted to increase my chances of becoming pregnant.

We had six unfertilized and unused eggs. Those eggs had been
outside of my body past the allotted time. Proper fertilization to

produce life with those eggs was highly unlikely. I did not care. I did not give a second of thought to it. I wanted more. I created life, knowing in my heart of hearts that I was creating a life that would be "abnormal," life that doctors would not implant into my body, life that was going to die.

I made a mistake. I put my desire to have a baby before my values and beliefs. I second-guessed God. The Bible tells us that God loves us with an everlasting love. He casts out our sins and mistakes as far as the east is from the west. He remembers them no more. If we confess our sins and mistakes to God, he removes them entirely from his mind. We no longer need to feel guilty or shameful about the past. Just as the story of the prodigal son, in the midst of our disobedience and running, God is faithful and merciful. He embraces us and restores us. God forgives!

⁓

Dear God,

I confess to you my mistakes, my worries, and my anxieties. I know you have everything worked out for those who love you. Thank you for removing my sins. Help me forgive myself. Amen.

WHAT DO YOU THINK?

When have you second-guessed God?

Describe a time that greed caused pain and hurt. Have you forgiven yourself?

PAST HAUNTINGS

Brothers and sisters, I do not consider myself yet to
have taken hold of it. But one thing I do: Forgetting
what is behind and straining toward what is ahead.
—Philippians 3:13

We have all made unwise choices. We have all made mistakes.
No one except Jesus is blameless or without fault. The book of
Numbers shares the story of Moses leading the Israelites around
the wilderness for forty years because of one bad decision, and
that one wrong decision kept the people, including Moses, from
entering the Promised Land.

> So Moses took the staff from the Lord's presence,
> just as he commanded him. He and Aaron
> gathered the assembly together in front of the rock
> and Moses said to them, "Listen, you rebels, must
> we bring you water out of this rock?" Then Moses
> raised his arm and struck the rock twice with
> his staff. Water gushed out, and the community
> and their livestock drank. But the Lord said to
> Moses and Aaron, "Because you did not trust in
> me enough to honor me as holy in the sight of the
> Israelites, you will not bring this community into
> the land I give them." (Numbers 20:9–12).

Can you imagine how Moses felt?

In another biblical example, Peter, one of the twelve disciples, denied that he knew Jesus three times. The Bible tells us that his mistake affected his emotional state. "And he went outside and wept bitterly" (Luke 22:62). He felt shame. He felt guilty about what he had said—his denial of knowing Jesus.

Have past mistakes contributed to your infertility journey? Jesus promises to forgive us if we confess our sins. He will forget our sins completely. However, that poor choice and that mistake is still a sin. Sin has consequences. It can be a physical denial like Moses or an emotional setback like Peter.

God forgives. We must forgive ourselves, accept the outcome of our choices, and learn from our mistakes. God knew the decisions we were going to make even before we knew it. Be filled with his glory and his peace—and know that he has forgiven you.

> As far as the east is from the west, so far has he removed our transgressions from us. (Psalm 103:12)

~

Dear God,

Please forgive me for my past mistakes. I thank you for your mercy and forgiveness. Help me use my past mistakes to help others. Amen.

WHAT DO YOU THINK?

Think about a time you made a poor decision. Are you still dwelling on that poor choice—or have you forgiven yourself?

What have you learned from your poor choices? How can that help others?

FIFTY BEATS

God's Nudge

All these blessings will come on you and accompany
you if you obey the Lord your God.
—Deuteronomy 28:2

Have you ever felt unsettled? Has your heart started pumping so fast when a particular opportunity arises? Have you felt unsure about something and cannot seem to shake it? Do you ignore the feeling? Do you assume it is nerves or anxiety? God tells us to be still. He tells us to listen for his voice. He directs our path. God's nudge is not comfortable. It is a feeling of unrest. It can weigh us down until our attention turns to him.

God nudged me. Two years after the birth of our twins, we began the treatment to unfreeze our remaining embryo and transfer it back into my body for our third child. I had started the medication protocol, we had secured a babysitter to watch the twins, and my husband had requested time off of work. Everything was going according to our plan. However, every time I stepped into church, the nudge of stopping the medication and the nudge to wait for the embryo transfer consumed my thoughts. I thought it was my anxiety. I thought it was my fear of a failed treatment. It could not be God. He wanted us to give this living embryo a chance of life as much as we did. Still, for weeks, that small voice kept saying, "No. Stop. Not now."

The transfer date finally arrived. It was the day the doctors would transfer the embryo into my body. I continued to hear the voice, but I continued to ignore it. I continued to feel unrest. The doctor said that the embryo appeared normal. My womb was in a pristine condition to support a baby. Everything was perfect. The transfer was a success.

Six weeks later, I lost the baby. I miscarried. I was devastated. What if I had listened to that voice? Had God been nudging me in a different direction to avoid heartbreak? Why did I not listen?

Listening to God is hard when we have made up our minds, when we have a plan, and when we want to be in control.

> He says, "Be still, and know that I am God." (Psalm 46:10).

When we listen to God and obey him, we will have his perfect peace. We will not feel unsettled. There will be no more anxious thoughts or fear. He will quiet our souls.

> Yes, my soul, find rest in God; my hope comes from him. (Psalm 62:5)

God nudges us often; we have to stop running our agenda and just be still.

~

Dear God,

Thank you for caring about me so much that you provide little nudges here and there to guide me in your direction. Help me listen to that voice even when it is difficult. Thank you for loving me. Amen.

WHAT DO YOU THINK?

*I*s God nudging you?

*W*hat is getting in the way of you hearing God?

When You Wish upon a Star

Take delight in the Lord, and he will give
you the desires of your heart.
—Psalm 37:4

God will give you the desires of your heart. Isn't that a remarkable promise? I pondered that verse when we transferred our frozen embryo. God knew my desire to complete our family with a third child. This desire was nothing new to God. The heart's desire to have a baby is part of the way God structured the world. Proverbs tells us that the barren womb is one of four things that will never satisfy us. It will never be enough.

The doctor unfroze the embryo before implantation. A picture of the embryo was put up on the screen. It looked like a circle with more than fifty little circles inside of it. According to the doctor, it was perfect. The transfer took place, and ten days later, God fulfilled my desire. I was pregnant.

I was thrilled. I knew that if I trusted in God, he would give me my desire. But at six weeks pregnant, things began to take a turn for the worse. At six weeks and four days, the baby's heart stopped beating. Miscarriage. I had lost my little one. What happened to my heart's desire?

My heart was aching. Nothing is impossible with God, so why did he not strengthen my baby's heartbeat? Why did he allow my baby to die? There is always a good reason that God denies our prayer requests. Perhaps God uses these moments to protect us and to refine us. Have we put the desire, the need for a baby, before God?

> I, the Lord your God, am a jealous God. (Exodus 20:5)

David tells us to take delight in the Lord and commit all that we have to him. Delight is to experience joy in his presence. Commit means to entrust everything to the Lord. We must believe that God knows our desires better than we do. By trusting in him, he will work out what is best for us. His ways and his desires for us are so much grander than we could ever imagine. Delight and commit yourself to the Lord, and your desires will start lining up with God's desires for your life—and nothing can beat that!

~

Dear Father,

Thank you for listening to my needs and desires. Help me stay focused on your Word and live out my life trusting in your great promises. Amen.

WHAT DO YOU THINK?

What are your desires?

Has God denied a prayer request? If so, what did you do next? Have you sought out the reason why he might have denied it?

BE SPECIFIC

And pray in the Spirit on all occasions with
all kinds of prayers and requests.
—Ephesians 6:18

How do you approach prayer? The Bible tells us that prayer is a direct source of communication with God. Think of prayer as talking with a good friend or talking with a family member. God is our heavenly Father, and he wants us to know him. He wants to speak to us. He craves a relationship with us just as we desire connections on Earth. We should be able to talk freely with God and to God.

So how do we pray? The disciples asked Jesus this exact question. Matthew tells us we should model our prayers after the Lord's Prayer:

> Our Father in heaven, hallowed be your name,
> your kingdom come, your will be done, on earth
> as it is in heaven. Give us today our daily bread.
> And forgive us our debts, as we also have forgiven
> our debtors. And lead us not into temptation, but
> deliver us from the evil one. (Matthew 6:9–13)

In *Prayer: Experiencing Awe and Intimacy with God,* Timothy Keller states,

> Each prayer such as the one that Jesus gave to his disciples, should contain four aspects: adoration, confession, praise and thanksgiving, and supplication, focusing on the needs of others and ourselves.[12]

I spoke daily with God during my frozen embryo cycle. I prayed that God would give our family a third child. I prayed that I would become pregnant. God answered my prayer. I achieved a pregnancy. However, the pregnancy only lasted six short weeks before I miscarried. Did my prayer not work? No. God heard my prayer. He answered my prayer. I did get pregnant. I was not specific enough in my prayer. I only asked him to achieve a pregnancy. I did not ask for a healthy pregnancy. I did not ask for a live birth in nine months. I was too general in my prayer.

God cares about our specific prayers. He wants to hear from us. He wants us to ask questions and take *all* of our concerns to him. He is interested in every detail of our lives—big or small. We should expect an answer to our specific prayers. Sometimes the answer will be "yes," sometimes the answer will be "no," and often the answer is "not yet."

> "Ask and it will be given to you; seek and you will find; knock and the door will be opened to you. For everyone who asks receives; the one who seeks finds; and to the one who knocks, the door will be opened. Which of you, if your son asks for bread, will give him a stone? Or if he asks for fish, will give him a snake? If you, then, though you are evil, know how to give good gifts to your children, how much more will your Father in heaven give good gifts to those who ask him!" (Matthew 7:7-11).

Pray. Pray hard, pray specifically, and pray without ceasing. God wants to hear from you!

~

Dear God,

I know you want to hear every detail of my life. Encourage me to share everything with you: my troubles, my praises, and my specific requests. Thank you for listening to me. Amen.

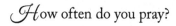

WHAT DO YOU THINK?

*H*ow often do you pray?

*A*re your prayers general or specific?

*W*hat are you specifically praying for now?

JOY!

Weeping may stay for the night, but
rejoicing comes in the morning.
—Psalm 30:5

I was thrilled when my frozen embryo implanted—and when I read the positive result on my home pregnancy test. I had waited two years for this moment. I could not wait to meet my little one. I would finally feel complete.

At six weeks pregnant, I had my first ultrasound. The doctors wanted to measure the heart rate to be sure it was least one hundred beats per minute. The baby's heartbeat was beating at fifty beats per minute. A miscarriage was most likely going to happen. We were devastated.

That night, I had a dream. In that dream, I saw a little girl with red, curly hair, pale skin, and lots of freckles. She was around the age of six. Over and over again, she assured me that everything was going to be okay. She told me that she was happy and that we would meet in heaven. She said she loved me and that her name was Joy. I woke up suddenly and knew I was no longer pregnant. My little girl had gone to be with Jesus.

My heart was breaking, but I took comfort in the fact that God had given me that dream. He provided closure and a feeling that everything was going to be okay. I do not know why God chose to take her from us so soon, but I am confident that I will meet her in heaven. I will never forget her. Her life was and still is important. She will forever be my Joy baby.

~

Dear God,

Please be with those families who have or will suffer a miscarriage. I know that every life is precious to you and that all children will have a special place in heaven. Give me the strength and courage to move past the weeping and have joy in knowing I will meet my little one someday. Amen.

WHAT DO YOU THINK?

If you suffered a miscarriage, have you named that child? Do you even want to give that child a name—or will it bring you more pain?

How have you remembered a lost loved one?

GOD'S OWN SON

Jesus called out with a loud voice, "Father, into your hands I commit my spirit." When he had said this, he breathed his last.
—Luke 23:46

My mom is the hospitality coordinator at a funeral home. She sees all types of death: natural causes, sickness, suicide, and tragic circumstances. She sees men, women, and children—old and young. They are all different, all sad, and all with a unique life story. The one thing they all have in common is the outpouring of love and support from family and friends. Most funeral homes host a visitation where friends and family can give their condolences to the family, bring a meal and flowers for comfort, and talk about the memories of the deceased. A visitation and funeral can help heal the soul and bring closure. A visitation and funeral can offer a shoulder to cry on and a way to show support to those suffering the loss.

All death is hard. All death is sad. I experienced a death of a child through my miscarriage. There was a unique person with a unique set of traits and DNA who perished. There was a heartbeat that stopped beating. The hard part of a miscarriage is that there is no obituary. There is no visitation. There is no funeral. The support given can hurt more than heal. Phrases such as "At least you can get pregnant," "Pregnancy will happen again," or "It was too early and not a real baby" can sting. My miscarriage was a baby, a loving child of God who I could picture playing on the playground and giving hugs and kisses to at night. I loved that child.

If you are experiencing heartbreak and sadness over a miscarriage, I am sorry. I understand and feel your pain. God understands too. We seem to forget that God lost a child. His Son, Jesus, died. The Bible states that darkness covered the land for three hours after his immediate death. All nature was mourning the death of God's son.

When we suffer a loss, God is crying and weeping alongside us. He sees our tears and feels our pain. He promises we will see our loved ones again.

> After that, we who are still alive and are left will
> be caught up together with them in the clouds to
> meet the Lord in the air. And so we will be with
> the Lord forever. (1 Thessalonians 4:17)

In the meantime, my husband and I have created a memory box of cards and ultrasound pictures. We have a piece of jewelry to symbolize our child's presence and have given her the name Joy. I cannot wait to meet her in heaven!

———

Dear God,

It is so awesome to know that you chose me to be a parent even if my baby was never entirely in my hands. Hold me close and give me the strength to move forward. Help me rely on the hope that I will meet my loved ones in heaven. Amen.

WHAT DO YOU THINK?

If you experienced a miscarriage, have you symbolized his or her life in a way to remember it?

How do you handle grief?

A Time to Laugh

Blessed are you who weep now, for you will laugh.
—Luke 6:21

One of my favorite movies is *My Best Friend's Wedding*. Toward the end of the film, there is a line that makes me smile every time I hear it. "But, by God, there will be laughing."[13] The actress, Julia Roberts, smiles, laughs, and gets up to dance. Life is good again.

Laughing and dancing may be far from your radar these days. If you are in a spot of weeping and crying because of infertility, it is okay. You are not alone. The Bible records Jesus crying on two separate occasions: one from the death of his friend Lazarus (John 11:35) and the other time is recorded in Luke 19 when the people of the city reject him.

> A time to weep and a time to laugh, a time to mourn and a time to dance. (Ecclesiastes 3:4)

Now is your time to cry and grieve. God tells us that when there is a valley, a mountain is right around the corner. Rely on God's promise of his power and his courage to pull you back to the top. Seek professional help—or speak to a pastor or a counselor. Find people who can bring Christ's message of hope and strength into your healing.

God promises us that we will laugh again.

> He will yet fill your mouth with laughter and your
> lips with shouts of joy. (Job 8:21)

—

Dear Lord,

You tell us that there is a time for everything. Please comfort me during my time of sadness and despair. Help me rely on your strength and your promises. Please provide the support and resources to find Christian help and guidance as I search for my laugh again. Amen.

WHAT DO YOU THINK?

What has helped you during your times of despair?

How can you get your laughter back?

HAPPY BIRTHDAY!

However many years anyone may live, let them enjoy them all.
—Ecclesiastes 11:8

September 1, 2016. My little girl would have been turning four years old on this exact date. I am sure she would have wanted everything princess for this birthday. I imagine her red, wavy hair and freckled face, bringing doughnuts into her preschool class as everyone sings "Happy Birthday."

But the reality is that she is not turning four here on earth. There will be no princesses or bringing doughnuts to her classroom. There will be no laughing or squeals as she runs down the steps to open presents. My little one did not make it out of the womb. Her heart stopped beating at six weeks and four days. Tiny as she was at the time, that baby was mine. I will always remember her and the day she was to be born.

God loves celebrations, and I have to believe that every year that she would have had a birthday on earth, she is celebrating it in heaven. I imagine that she is celebrating it with our loved ones who have passed away, with the angels singing "Happy Birthday" in the background, and her gift is the greatest gift of all: a hug from Jesus himself.

I love you, little one, and I cannot wait to see you in heaven!

Dear God,

Death is hard. Help me treasure and celebrate the times I was able to spend with my loved ones and to know that I will see them once again in your presence. Amen.

WHAT DO YOU THINK?

*H*ow do you celebrate birthdays?

*D*o you celebrate birthdays of deceased family members? If so, how?

NO HEARTBEAT

I call on the Lord in my distress and he answers me.
—Psalm 120:1

I recently received a text from a very dear friend who was experiencing a miscarriage. Two weeks prior, we were celebrating her positive pregnancy test.

One in four women will experience a miscarriage.[14] Women are told not to share the news of a pregnancy before twelve weeks, just in case. Most miscarriages happen between six and ten weeks. So, because the announcement of pregnancy is not shared prior, women are then stuck with putting on a fake smile and pretending as if nothing happened. Women are dealing with the pain of a miscarriage alone. I know this pain. I know this sorrow. I know the guilt that perhaps I did something wrong to induce a miscarriage.

No one should have to go through a miscarriage alone. We need to be present for those going through this challenging time. We need to remember that precious life. We need to encourage others to speak out about their loss and guide them to God in his everlasting hope and love that he provides to the brokenhearted. Let us change society's standards of keeping miscarriages a secret and start celebrating and remembering the life that we will one day see again.

Bible Verses of Encouragement

Proverbs 3:5–6
Isaiah 41:10
John 14:27
John 16:33
Psalm 46:1–5
Psalm 55:22
1 Peter 5:7

~

Dear God,

Please help me as I comfort those grieving. Help me as I walk in this lonely time and to know that joy will come again. Amen.

WHAT DO YOU THINK?

*H*ave you ignored the pain of a miscarriage? If so, why?

*W*hen you told someone about your miscarriage, how did they respond? Did that response hurt or encourage you?

LEAN ON ME

Be devoted to one another in love. Honor
one another above yourselves.
—Romans 12:10

I have many friends and acquaintances who have struggled with
infertility, miscarriage, and stillborn. To this day, I cannot tell
you how these women are handling their heartbreak and loss.
They do not know of my raw emotions surrounding infertility. It
is as if these adverse circumstances in our lives did not happen.
Why are infertility and loss so difficult to discuss? Are we afraid
of being too vulnerable? Are we afraid of being judged? Are we
afraid of our feelings?

God created us to love one another just as he loves us. He
wants us to call on him when we are in need. He also provides
people in our lives at the right time to help us on our life journeys.

A friend loves at all times, and a brother is born
for a time of adversity. (Proverbs 17:17)

God desires us to have intimate and close relationships with
each other. We cannot do so unless we start asking questions
and being vulnerable ourselves. We need to dive deep into
conversations. We need to share our stories and help lead the

way. Let us take the initiative and go first, knowing that God will hold our hands.

———

Dear God,

Reaching out to people can be hard. You have called us to be intimate with each other and to lean on each other. Guide my conversations. Help me be more vulnerable. Help me be courageous and share my story. Amen.

WHAT DO YOU THINK?

*A*re you vulnerable with family and friends—or do you find yourself closed off and quiet?

What does courage look like to you?

WILL YOU HOLD MY HAND?

Therefore encourage one another and build each
other up, just as in fact you are doing.
—1 Thessalonians 5:11

Infertility affects one in eight couples,[15] yet it is a very private topic. No one talks about it. No one knows. My husband and I went through years of infertility trials. Our families had no idea. Appearance was more important than sharing a hardship. We wanted to give the impression that our marriage was perfect and that we were choosing to postpone children.

After the twins were born, we continued to keep our infertility woes under wraps. There were ample times to explain our hardship. We were asked regularly if twins ran in the family. Still, we kept our fertility procedures to ourselves. After my miscarriage, one of the lowest parts of my infertility struggle, I began sharing "our story."

To my amazement, no one judged us. Not one person questioned us about our decisions. The complete opposite happened. Others started sharing their failed pregnancy attempts, their miscarriages, and their fertility issues. My fear of being judged went out the window. The more people I told, the better I felt. I realized that many couples were also battling hardships and that God was using our infertility story to help others.

Greater love has no one than this: to lay down one's life for one's friends. (John 15:13)

We can exercise this kind of love by listening, encouraging, being a shoulder to lean on, and sharing our personal stories.

Are you keeping your infertility a secret? Are you afraid of what others might think? Are you fearful of not appearing perfect? It is during hardship that we need to share with others. We need to encourage each other. Be gutsy, go first, and start talking!

~

Dear God,

Thank you so much for supportive friends and family. They may not understand my infertility situation, but knowing that they will listen is so important. Help me see that you are also my friend and that I can talk to you about anything. Thank you for loving me so much. Amen.

WHAT DO YOU THINK?

*D*o you fear others will judge your decisions? How can you move past that fear?

*H*ow can your infertility struggles help others?

I CAN'T GET NO SATISFACTION

WHOM DO YOU SERVE?

No one can serve two masters. Either you will
hate the one and love the other, or you will be
devoted to the one and despise the other.
—Matthew 6:24

Proverbs states that "there are three things that are never satisfied, four that never say, 'Enough!': the grave, the barren womb, land... and fire" (Proverbs 30:15-16). An empty womb is one of the four things the verse mentions. Having a third baby became my obsession. It took over my life. I spent all of my time and energy thinking and talking about it.

The desire for and obsession with a third child became even stronger after my miscarriage. I contemplated ways of fulfilling that desire. I added my name to an adoption list. I had my husband take a woman's fertility drug. I started saving for another round of IVF. I lived and breathed thinking about another baby.

The Bible tells us that we must overcome our fixations. God alone should be our master. We must focus our eyes on him and serve him alone.

> Jesus replied: "Love the Lord your God with all
> your heart and with all your soul and with all your
> mind." (Matthew 22:37).

We must devote our minds, souls, and hearts to God. This—and only this—will slow the obsession of our fleshly desires and truly center us on what God would desire for our lives. That is where we will find the peace he has so greatly promised us.

～

Dear God,

Life can be hard when I want something so much. Help me focus my thoughts, time, and efforts on serving you during my time of need. Amen.

What Do You Think?

Who or what is your master?

How can you overcome your obsessions?

CAN YOU COUNT YOUR BLESSINGS?

One of them, when he saw that he was healed,
came back, praising God in a loud voice.
—Luke 17:15

I love the look of the farmhouse style, especially the wooden word signs. The other day, I found a hand-carved sign that said: "We Are Blessed." It matches my black and white bedroom décor perfectly, and it looks great on my nightstand.

My husband and I were blessed. We had three-year-old twin girls, had just moved closer to family, and had recently purchased a house. We had our health—and my husband had a job where I could stay at home—but I was still dwelling on the loss of my baby. Months before, I had suffered a miscarriage from our one and only frozen embryo. It devastated me. I wanted another baby and could not think of anything else. It became a fixation. It was all I talked about with my husband. I had my daughters praying for a "baby in my belly." I could not enjoy the present situation or my current blessings. It felt as if I were in a deep hole, and the more I tried to climb out of it, the more the dirt kept pulling me back in. I was going deeper and deeper into depression.

During that time, I came across the story of Jesus healing the ten lepers. After the miraculous healing, nine of the men immediately forgot to thank Jesus. Only one returned his healing with gratitude. Only one remembered to say thank you. Was I becoming too entangled in my wants and needs that I forgot that God had provided my miracle twin babies? Did I forget the blessing of my family? Did I remember to thank God?

My "We Are Blessed" sign is the perfect reminder that I am indeed blessed. There is always something to be thankful for—even in the midst of our suffering. God will use that grateful heart to teach us more about him.

~

Dear Lord,

I pray that you take away my obsessions. Help me center my life on the blessings you have already provided. Your grace is enough. Amen.

WHAT DO YOU THINK?

What is consuming your life?

Is there a time you forgot to thank God?

Do you only remember God during your struggles—or do you also remember God when things are going well?

WHAT WILL SATISFY YOU?

Search me, God, and know my heart; test me and
know my anxious thoughts. See if there is any offensive
way in me, and lead me in the way everlasting.
—Psalm 139:23–24

"When are you going to have another baby?" friends would ask.
I had just experienced a miscarriage and used our last remaining
embryo, but I desperately desired another child. Was it even
possible? Could I have another baby? I found myself in the midst
of childless couples and larger families. I was under the umbrella
of secondary infertility.

Secondary infertility affects more than three million women
in the United States.[16] These couples experience the joy of a
child, but the heartbreak of not being able to conceive a sibling.
Physicians downplay secondary infertility by saying, "keep
trying." Also, those with secondary infertility usually receive less
support from family and friends. Secondary infertility is very
lonely. Helane S. Rosenberg and Yakov M. Epstein, authors of
Getting Pregnant When You Thought You Couldn't, state, "You have
lost your membership in the primary infertility group by attaining
the dream. Yet you feel you do not really belong to the world of
the fertile."[17]

There is a sense of guilt that couples with secondary infertility
should be happy with the one child God has given them. Proverbs

tell us that four things will never satisfy us. One is an empty womb. The desire to have a child is a God-given desire. He gave it to us, and because he gave us this desire, he will see us through it. He will comfort us when things do not go exactly as we had hoped and planned.

> Let us throw off everything that hinders and the sin that so easily entangles. And let us run with perseverance the race marked out for us, fixing our eyes on Jesus, the pioneer and perfecter of faith. (Hebrews 12:1–2)

Through prayer and daily devotions, God has helped me overcome my desires. However, there are times when I will read a pregnancy post on social media—or see a mother holding her newborn child—and think, *Why not me?* Paul says it best in Corinthians:

> I was given a thorn in my flesh, a messenger of Satan, to torment me. Three times I pleaded with the Lord to take it away from me. But he said to me, "My grace is sufficient for you, for my power is made perfect in weakness." Therefore I will boast all the more gladly about my weaknesses, so that Christ's power may rest on me. That is why, for Christ's sake, I delight in weaknesses, in insults, in hardships, in persecutions, in difficulties. For when I am weak, then I am strong. (2 Corinthians 12:7–10)

Our hardship and weakness allow us to rely on God for strength. God's grace is enough.

Dear God,

My desire for a child is so strong. Hold me up in this time of struggle. Be with me, so I do not feel alone. Guide my heart and mind so that the seeds of jealousy and bitterness do not take root. Help me know that your grace is all I need. Amen.

WHAT DO YOU THINK?

What are the four things Proverbs mentions that will never satisfy us?

How can you support someone going through secondary infertility? What sort of support would you want if faced with this circumstance?

WHEN IS ENOUGH ENOUGH?

He gives strength to the weary and increases the power of
the weak. Even youths grow tired and weary, and young men
stumble and fall; but those who hope in the Lord will renew
their strength. They will soar on wings like eagles; they will
run and not grow weary, they will walk and not be faint.
—Isaiah 40:29–31

We do not need a devotional or a counselor to tell us when to stop
"trying" to conceive. We know when we have had enough failed
pregnancy attempts and fertility treatments. But enough does not
mean giving up. Doing nothing is giving up. Enough implies a
change to our plans, a change in our course of action. Times of
change are necessary.

> Let us not become weary in doing good, for at the
> proper time we will reap a harvest if we do not
> give up. (Galatians 6:9)

God tells us to never give up on him or his miracles. God's
power and strength will never weaken. He is never too tired or
too busy to see us through it. God's Word promises that he will
strengthen us to move on.

Sometimes, we must change our patterns or the way we
think—or find a whole new path. This could mean trying a

new fertility treatment, starting the process of adoption, or being content with no children. He promises to strengthen us to move past life's difficulties. He promises to love us. He wants the very best for us. We must persevere trusting in God always.

> I press on toward the goal to win the prize for which God has called me heavenward in Christ Jesus. (Philippians 3:14)

Do not give up on him because he will never give up on us!

~

Dear God,

Life can be so difficult at times. Sometimes, I want to quit and to walk away, but your Word tells us to hang tough and hang tight to your promises. Help me live in those promises and lean on you when I am too weak to go on. Thank you, Lord, for loving me so much. Amen.

WHAT DO YOU THINK?

What have you had enough of?

What plans do you need to change?

DEFEATED, DEPLETED, AND DISCOURAGED

Watch and pray so that you will not fall into temptation.
The spirit is willing, but the flesh is weak.
—Mark 14:38

Have you ever disagreed with a post on social media? Did you respond to the post? What was the result? I assume that you got bombarded with answers of "how wrong you are" and "how dare you think that way." We, as a society, do not know how to disagree anymore. We tend to partner with those who believe what we agree with, and we "unfriend" those who do not agree with us. We have become narrow-minded with our viewpoints and think "our way" is the best way and the only way.

So, what do you do and how do you act when you disagree with God? How do you respond when you disagree with your circumstances or what is happening in your life? Jesus has set the example for us when we feel defeated, depleted, and discouraged.

After the Last Supper, Jesus and his disciples when to the Garden of Gethsemane to pray.

> Going a little farther, he fell to the ground and prayed that if possible the hour might pass from him. "Abba, Father," he said "everything is possible for you. Take this cup from me." (Mark 14:35-36).

Jesus begged God to use his power over his purpose. His soul ached to change the circumstance. He also could not sleep as his disciples did. His concerns, questions, and pleadings kept him up at night.

The scripture does not stop there.

"Yet not what I will, but what you will."
(Mark 14:36).

Even in his most desperate and powerless moment, Jesus showed us that he trusted in his Father God. He trusted God's character. He trusted God over his present circumstance. When he was desperate, defeated, and depleted, he kept on praying. He persevered in his prayers.

An angel from heaven appeared to him and strengthened him. And being in anguish, he prayed more earnestly, and his sweat was like drops of blood falling to the ground. (Luke 22:43–44)

We must choose to trust God in our present circumstance— even when we disagree. God can get us through anything. He knows the outcome, and he assures us that there is victory through him, the victory of eternal life.

~

Dear God,

I cannot see the future, and I do not know how it will turn out. Help me put my trust in you. Help me persevere in prayer. Help me continue to hope and trust that you have my entire life in your hands. Thank you for loving me so much. Amen.

What Do You Think?

Have you ever disagreed with God? If so, what did you disagree with?

How can you change your attitude? What is God trying to teach you through your present circumstances?

THE MIRACLE
OF LIFE

BE QUIET ALREADY

My son, if you accept my words and store up my commands
within you, turning your ear to wisdom and applying your heart
to understanding—indeed, if you call out for insight and cry
aloud for understanding, and if you look for it as for silver and
search for it as for hidden treasure, then you will understand
the fear of the Lord and find the knowledge of God.
—Proverbs 2:1–5

God speaks to his children through the Bible, the Holy Spirit,
and godly people. His voice can be audible, but most times, he
breathes life into our thoughts. It might appear as an unsettled
feeling, our palms might become sweaty, or our hearts may start
to beat a little bit faster. How do we know if it is God or our
anxiety? We are to "take captive every thought to make it obedient
to Christ" (2 Corinthians 10:5).

When my husband and I were in the midst of medications
during our frozen embryo transfer, I was not at peace. I felt
uneasy. I felt as if I should not be moving forward with the
fertility treatment. I ignored the feeling. I thought it was my
anxiety. I believed we were doing the correct thing. I thought
we were following God's will. Six weeks after the transfer, I
miscarried. Had God been talking to me beforehand? Was he
trying to prevent heartache? Would we have had this child if we
had waited?

Fast-forward three years later, and my husband and I decided to pursue IVF for a third child. Again, I kept struggling with the IVF decision. I was not at peace with the treatment even though I strongly desired another child. Doctors told us IVF was our only option to conceive, and they said we had to move forward if we wanted another child. I ignored the unsettled feeling.

I took my first dose of IVF medication the same day as my weekly Bible study. It was the story of Judah and Tamar. Judah was the son of Jacob. He had three sons. The oldest son married Tamar. He died and left Tamar childless. It was custom at that time for Tamar to marry the next son in line so she could bear a child. These two sons were not men of God. They found ways to avoid impregnating Tamar. God killed them.

What did Tamar do next? She prostituted herself and slept with her father-in-law, Judah. Most Bible scholars believe that Tamar was desperate to be part of this family line. God opened my eyes to notice something different. I observed a woman getting older, with no husband and no children. She was desperate for a child. She tried everything, including sleeping with her father-in-law. She did not have faith that God would provide her with offspring. Was I doing the same thing? Was I controlling the outcome instead of letting God be God?

It was right then that God pointed me to the book of Luke.

> Even Elizabeth your relative is going to have a child in her old age, and she who was said to be unable to conceive is in her sixth month. For no word from God will ever fail. (Luke 1:36–37)

God had spoken. This time, I chose to listen and canceled the treatment.

> And the peace of God, which transcends all understanding, will guard your hearts and your minds in Christ Jesus. (Philippians 4:7)

I no longer had that unsettled feeling. God's peace was surrounding me.

~

Dear God,

It can be hard to hear your voice with all the chatter of the world. Please be very clear and help me follow your direction—even if it might not be the answer I am seeking at that moment. Help us trust you completely. Amen.

WHAT DO YOU THINK?

Have you ignored God?

What are you trying to control?

Do you feel God's peace and presence in all areas of your life? In what areas of your life do you need more of God's peace and presence?

Anything Is Possible

Jesus looked at them and said, "With man this is
impossible, but with God all things are possible."
—Matthew 19:26

Nothing is impossible with God. Do you believe that? Do you
think that—no matter what the doctors say about your infertility
diagnosis—nothing is impossible with God?

On April 20, 2013, God told us to stop another round of IVF.
My husband and I decided to stop all talk about a third child
for one calendar year. For one year, there would be no mention
of fertility treatments, no researching information on adoption,
and no putting our names on an embryo adoption list. Nothing.
Absolutely nothing. It was difficult. Just because we stopped
pursuing treatments did not mean that my heart changed. I still
thought about and wanted a third child. How were we going to
conceive another child when doctors told us that we had less than
a 1 percent chance of conceiving on our own?

The next few months were busy for our family of four. We
sold our home, moved across the country, and started new jobs.
My monthly cycle was late. No big deal. With all the stress of
moving, I was not surprised. In the past, when I was "late," I
would take a home pregnancy test. It would read negative, and the
very next day, my cycle would start. I took the home pregnancy
test, but this time, the test showed a positive result: two lines. I

scrambled for another test stick, and this time, it read "Pregnant." Nothing is impossible with God!

Doctors had told us that we had less than a 1 percent chance of conceiving on our own. God does not deal with percentages. God is the same yesterday, today, and forever. On May 22, 2014, approximately one year later—when talks of a third child would have resumed—we welcomed Saul Matthew into the world. Saul means "desired" and "prayed for," and Matthew means "a gift from God." My impossible situation turned into a reality. God has no limits as to what he can do!

—

Dear God,

Thank you for your blessings. Thank you for your power. Your name is higher than any other—and what you can do is astounding. Help me trust you and know that nothing is impossible with you. Amen.

WHAT DO YOU THINK?

*W*hy do you think God makes us go through impossible situations?

*W*hat feels impossible to you right now?

GOD: THE GIVER OF LIFE

Before I formed you in the womb I knew you,
before you were born I set you apart.
—Jeremiah 1:5

Thirty-five weeks and four days, thirty-nine weeks and six days, and six weeks and four days are how long I carried each of my babies. Full term is considered forty weeks, ten months. I did not carry any of my babies to full term.

We named my six-weeks-four-day-old unborn baby Joy. God's Word states that there is a plan for everything and everyone, including the unborn. God does not put one life ahead of another life. No one is greater on earth than Jesus. In Exodus, God gave the people rules and regulations to follow. He stated that if a man kills another man, then the man should flee his countryside. And if a man kills an unborn child, then his punishment should be death (Exodus 21:22–25).

God values the life of the unborn. Jeremiah 1 emphasizes God's relationship with an unborn child. God views us at conception. Conception is the fertilization between a woman's egg and a man's sperm. According to God, our life span is from conception until death—not birth until death.

How do you view life? How do you view IVF? Are you creating more life than you plan to use? Are you terminating a life because of chromosomal abnormalities? Are you disregarding lives because there is abundance? These are tough questions for those going through fertility treatments, but should they be? God's Word makes it very clear. He is very specific when it comes to the life of all people. My baby Joy is a life that God created. All life is good.

—

Dear God,

You are the giver of life. Thank you for all life. Thank you for the sacrifice of your one and only Son. Thank you for loving me so much. Amen.

WHAT DO YOU THINK?

When do you believe life starts?

How do you view life as it pertains to fertility treatments?

Apples,
Oranges &
Bananas

Is My Faith Sufficient?

He said to her, "Daughter, your faith has healed you.
Go in peace, and be freed from your suffering."
—Mark 5:34

I was in a passion play for many years at my home church. I always played the woman Jesus healed by the touching of his robe. This woman had an incurable condition, causing her to have an ongoing menstrual cycle. By Jewish standards, she was considered unclean and could not touch Jesus. On one particular day, she stepped out in faith and grabbed his robe. Immediately she was healed. Her faith was stronger than a custom or a law, and Jesus restored her to good health.

Why is Jesus not healing me of my infertility? Am I not praying hard enough? Am I not faithful enough? I look all around, and everyone seems to be having babies: the unbelievers, the high school teenagers, and the unwed mothers. I am doing everything God's way, so what is happening? When will my prayers work? When will they be enough? I was angry. I was depressed. Why was this happening to me?

The fall of sin has put this hardship and sorrowful fate on women. Genesis states that conceiving would be difficult.

To the woman he said, "I will make your pains in childbearing very severe; with painful labor you will give birth to children." (Genesis 3:16).

In *God of All Comfort*, Judy Gann writes,

> God can remove our illness and change our circumstance in an instant. Until then, we can rest in the fact that our illnesses are part of his good purpose for our lives. God truly uses all things.[18]

God used infertility to mold me into the person I was meant to be. God used my infertility to nurture my Christian faith. Infertility made my marriage stronger. Infertility made me appreciate my blessings, and it also encouraged me to help others battling the same hardships. The Lord used—and is using— my infertility to draw others closer to him. Is God using your condition to prove his love and grace to someone else? Our faith is enough. It truly is.

~

Dear God,

Thank you for being with me in my current situation. Help me trust your timing, your power, and your will. Amen.

What Do You Think?

After the fall of sin, God told women that they would have sorrow in childbearing and painful labor. Why do you think God cursed women with this? How does that make you feel?

What have you learned from your infertility journey?

What Fruit Are You Eating?

*But the fruit of the Spirit is love, joy, peace, forbearance,
kindness, goodness, faithfulness, gentleness, and self-control.*
—Galatians 5:22–23

Infertility is a tough road. God tells us in his Word that life is not going to be easy. We will experience valleys. We will suffer hardship. We will experience heartache. But God also promises that if we follow him, he will guide our path. His light will shine forth. It will be a light that others will see. It will be a chance for us to teach others about his power, his goodness, and his mercies. The Bible states that we reap what we have sown. What fruit have you discovered because of your infertility?

> Love. "Love the Lord your God with all your heart and with all your soul and with all your mind and with all your strength. The second is this: 'Love your neighbor as yourself.' There is no commandment greater than these" (Mark 12:30–31).

> Joy. "Rejoice always, pray continually, give thanks in all circumstances; for this is God's will for you in Christ Jesus" (1 Thessalonians 5:16–18).

Peace. "And the peace of God, which transcends all understanding, will guard your hearts and your minds in Christ Jesus" (Philippians 4:7).

Patience. "Be still before the Lord and wait patiently for him" (Psalm 37:7).

Kindness. "Be kind and compassionate to one another, forgiving each other, just as in Christ God forgave you" (Ephesians 4:32).

Goodness. "Do not be overcome by evil, but overcome evil with good" (Romans 12:21).

Faithfulness. "With man this is impossible, but with God all things are possible" (Matthew 19:26).

Gentleness. "Be wise in the way you act toward outsiders; make the most of every opportunity. Let your conversation be always full of grace, seasoned with salt, so that you may know how to answer everyone" (Colossians 4:5–6).

Self-Control. "No temptation has overtaken you except what is common to mankind. And God is faithful; he will not let you be tempted beyond what you can bear. But when you are tempted, he will also provide a way out so that you can endure it" (1 Corinthians 10:13).

~

Dear God,

Help me abide by the fruit of the Spirit. I praise you for your mercy, grace, and forgiving heart. Help me love like you. Amen.

WHAT DO YOU THINK?

What fruit of the Spirit resembles you the most?

What fruit of the Spirit are you lacking?

Expectations

Yes, my soul, find rest in God; my hope comes from him.
—Psalm 62:5

I never expected to be labeled infertile, but three years into our marriage, that was the exact word that defined us. I expected us to have a plethora of children. In fact, we even hoped pregnancy would happen on our wedding night!

We could not wait to be parents. We expected it to happen right away. It did not. So, we purchased an ovulation test, expecting it to happen. Again, another failed attempt. We then bought the most expensive ovulation kit because the more money you spend, the more accurate the testing will be, right? Again, it did not work. Next, we tried fertility drugs. Still, we expected it to work, yet it did not.

Month after month, year after year, we experienced this constant up-and-down emotional roller coaster—only to feel let down after another failed attempt. We did not expect that conceiving a child would be so hard. We did not expect that infertility was our road map. We did not expect that God would allow this to happen to us.

God's answer comes from his perspective and is not always in line with our expectations. God knows our futures. He knows the whole story, and a little hiccup in the road can lead to even bigger expectations, as it did for us. We never expected twins. We never expected to become pregnant on our own after seven years of trying. We never expected to be holding our baby after doctors told us that we had less than a 1 percent chance of conceiving naturally. But it did happen. God expected it.

~

Dear God,

You have my entire future lined up. Help me put my trust entirely in you for all things. Amen.

WHAT DO YOU THINK?

*N*ame a time you were surprised.

*W*hat are your expectations?

*W*hy do we limit God's expectations for our lives?

What Is Your Road Map?

Do you not know that in a race all the runners run, but only
one gets the prize? Run in such a way as to get the prize.
—1 Corinthians 9:24

Have you ever taken a road trip? Did your travel require you to
change directions? Did you stay straight and on the same road the
entire time? Most likely, you turned right and left and went up
hills and down hills until you got to your anticipated destination.
Did it take a long time? The road trip probably took a bit longer
than a typical trip to the grocery store.

Most great destinations will take us thousands of miles with
many dips and turns along the way. With most great road trips,
the journey is usually where the most significant memories take
place. Do not get me wrong. Getting to the destination is a
great feeling, but going through the trials of getting there can
produce life-changing experiences that we will never forget. My
infertility road map had many zigzags (marriage, the heartache
of not conceiving, the blessing of twins, miscarriage, and finally
my miracle son).

What is your road map in life? How will you get from point A
to point B? Are you so focused on the ending that you are missing
the highlights along the way? Are you missing God's miracles?
God has not given us a map, a list of where to go and when to

go, but he has given us his Word. The Bible offers essential information on how to live.

> All scripture is God-breathed and is useful for teaching, rebuking, correcting and training in righteousness, so that the servant of God may be thoroughly equipped for every good work. (2 Timothy 3:16–17)

God never told us that our lives would be easy and straight down the road.

> I have told you these things, so that in me you may have peace. In this world you will have trouble. But take heart! I have overcome the world. (John 16:33)

He did promise us, however, that his plan is perfect and that he will be with us along the way. We will never be alone.

> God has said, 'Never will I leave you; never will I forsake you." (Hebrews 13:5).

God does not promise us a happily ever after, but he does promise us an eternal ever after. This is your great adventure. Make the most of it!

> Saddle up your horses. We've got a trail to blaze… Through the wild blue yonder of God's Amazing grace. Let's follow our leader into the Glorious unknown. This is the life like no other…This is the great adventure.[19]

Dear God,

Thank you for your perfect plan. Help me make wise decisions and take all things to you in prayer. Thank you for your everlasting miracles in my life and help me see the good in every which way I turn. Amen.

What Do You Think?

Describe your road map.

What stops along the way have been the most memorable?

How is God helping you get to your final destination?

EPILOGUE

(Bits and pieces of this story are from the above devotions. I shared this testimony at a Cherry Hills Christian Church Mothers of Preschoolers meeting.)

~

Expectations. We all have them, whether it is expecting a phone call from our husband to expecting a gift for our birthday. It is the unexpected situations that can cause our greatest joy and our greatest grief.

I never expected to be labeled infertile, but three years into our marriage, that was the exact word that defined us. My husband and I could not wait to be parents. In fact, we even hoped pregnancy would happen on our wedding night. We expected to conceive right away. It did not. So, we purchased an ovulation test, expecting it to happen shortly after that. Again, it did not. We then bought the most expensive ovulation kit because the more money you spend, the more accurate the testing will be, right? Again, another failed attempt. Next, we tried fertility drugs. Still, it did not work. Month after month, year after year, we experienced this constant up-and-down emotional roller coaster, only to feel let down after another failed attempt. We did not expect that conceiving a child would be so hard. We did not expect that infertility would be our road map. We did not expect that God would allow this to happen to us.

I was in a passion play for many years at my home church. I always played the woman whom Jesus healed by the touching of his robe. By Jewish standards, she was considered unclean and could not touch Jesus. One day, as Jesus was passing by, she stepped out in faith and grabbed his robe. Immediately she was healed. Her faith was stronger than a custom or a law, and Jesus restored her to good health. So why was Jesus not curing me of my infertility? Everywhere I turned, someone was announcing a pregnancy. Why was this happening to us? We both loved the Lord. We lived by his standards and strived to obey him, but month after month our prayers went unanswered.

I was bitter, angry, and depressed. My husband could not provide the one thing I so desperately wanted. Our marriage was struggling. Sex was becoming a chore. Where is this baby? When will my prayers work? In Corinthians, Paul asks the Lord to take away his affliction:

> But he said to me, "My grace is sufficient for you, for my power is made perfect in weakness." (2 Corinthians 12:9).

We finally decided that we needed to see a specialist. Our doctor had a soft demeanor that made us feel comfortable from the start. He wanted us to have a baby just as much as we wanted to have a baby. He walked us through the steps of our reproductive issues and then explained that in vitro fertilization (IVF) was our only option to achieve a pregnancy. We were excited. We finally had an answer with a solution. Our dream of having a baby was about to come true. He gave us paperwork to look over, and the treatment would begin in one month.

The paperwork contained numerous questions about our faith and beliefs, such as "When do you believe life begins?" and "What will you do with the extra embryos?" We were deeply concerned. What was IVF? Doctors needed to retrieve as many eggs from my body and fertilize them with my husband's sperm. The more fertilized, the better the chance of a successful pregnancy. My husband and I believe that life begins at conception. The Bible states, "For you created my inmost being; you knit me together in my mother's womb" (Psalms 139:13). Fertilization to us was conception. Were we driving ourselves into the lion's den?

As much as we wanted children and a family, we had to stop moving forward with IVF. We are on God's team, and that team views embryos as lives—not pieces of conception and not something to discard after use. We called the clinic and told them that we needed more time to think. We wanted to make the best decision for us and be sure it lined up with God's will and purpose.

We read and researched and read some more. My mind was on overload with the amount of stuff that is on the internet regarding infertility. What was true? What was untrue? My mind was spinning out of control. When we overthink, we tend to focus on adverse outcomes or problems that may arise. We keep circling our situation in hopes of gaining control over it and gaining control over our emotions. We spend too much energy playing out scenarios over and over in our heads that we lose focus on the one thing that matters the most: Jesus Christ.

I began to turn away from the internet and started turning my thoughts to Christ. I read the Bible, read Christian literature about IVF, talked with our pastor and marriage counselor, and prayed continually. After all that, we still felt God opening the door to IVF. However, the godly advice we received was specific. We could only create embryos that we were going to use. We had to overcome the pressure from doctors and the clinic staff to produce more. We accepted the fact that IVF might not be successful. God tells us that the fight might not be easy. There will be struggles along the way, but we must persevere.

> I press on toward the goal to win the prize for
> which God has called me heavenward in Christ
> Jesus. (Philippians 3:14)

We planned to fertilize ten eggs. We planned to use all ten embryos if fertilization occurred positively. On the day of my egg-retrieval surgery, the embryologist removed sixteen eggs from my body. Doctors fertilized our planned ten eggs. The other six eggs remained unused and unfertilized in the lab. Think of these remaining eggs as six menstrual cycles. One unfertilized egg releases in every cycle. The following day would determine the outcome of the ten fertilized embryos.

The next day came, and the news was grim. Out of the ten eggs that fertilized, only four were sustainable embryos and growing life. If these embryos implanted inside my body, four children were in our future. I was in panic mode. I did not plan for this. I was not happy with four embryos. I wanted more. The other embryos needed to remain in a petri dish for two more days before transferring them back into my body. Would they survive two more days? I needed a plan, and I needed it fast. Without consulting my husband or praying about it, I put my new plan into motion.

"What about those remaining six eggs in the lab?" I asked. "Can we fertilize those eggs now?" The eggs had been outside of my body past the allotted timeframe. Proper fertilization to produce life with those eggs was highly unlikely. I did not care. I did not give a second thought to it. I wanted more. I needed that baby.

The next morning, the doctors called with bad news. The last six eggs did not fertilize into life. In fact, doctors used the word "abnormal." What did that mean? Did I create life only to throw it away?

Trust in the Lord with all your heart and lean not
on your own understanding. (Proverbs 3:5)

Why did I compromise our plan? Why did I not consult my husband? Why did I not trust God?

Two days later, we prepared for the embryo transfer. This is it! I am finally going to be pregnant. All four embryos were still alive. One embryo was developing slowly, one was growing too fast, and two were precisely as they should be. Two were perfect embryos. Perfect. God's perfection at work. I asked to implant all four embryos. I did not want to leave any behind. The doctor only agreed to implant two embryos. We would freeze the remaining two for the future, to expand our family. Before the implantation process began, we were able to view the embryos on a television monitor. We saw two embryos with eight cells each. My babies. It is hard not to see life at its beginning when you view that.

The transfer went smoothly. Five weeks later, we had our first ultrasound appointment to see if we were indeed pregnant. We saw and heard two heartbeats, two strong heartbeats. We were pregnant with twins, and on October 2, 2009, our two little princesses were born.

However, I had made a mistake. I put my desire of having a baby before my values and beliefs. I second-guessed God. God only gives us what we can handle. He knows the result the entire time. If I had only just trusted in him instead of trying to take control of the situation, I could have avoided the guilt and shame that still shadows my life today. The Bible tells us that God loves us with an everlasting love. He casts out our sins and mistakes as far as the east is from the west. He remembers them no more. I may have consequences for past choices, but if I confess, God will remove these sins entirely from his mind!

Life was busy with twins, but not a day went by that I did not think about my frozen embryo, my baby at the fertility clinic. This was the embryo that was growing too fast. The one that was growing too slow did not survive, but I know I will see that baby in heaven.

Two years after the twins' birth, we began the treatment to unfreeze our one remaining embryo and transfer it back into my body. I started the medication protocol, we secured a babysitter to watch the girls during the procedure, and my husband requested time off from work. Everything was going according to our plan, but every time I stepped into church, the nudge to the stop the medication and the nudge to wait for the embryo transfer consumed my thoughts. I ignored it. I thought it was my anxiety. I thought it was my fear of a failed treatment. It could not be God. He wanted to give this living embryo a chance at life as much as we did. God knew my desire of completing our family with a third child, and his Word states that he will give us the desires of our heart. Yet, week after week, that still small voice kept saying, "No. Stop. Not now."

The transfer date finally arrived. It was the day the doctors would transfer the embryo into my body. I continued to hear the voice, but I continued to ignore it. I continued to feel unrest. A picture of the embryo was put up on the screen. It looked like a circle with more than fifty little circles inside of it. The embryo was growing. It was alive. The transfer took place, and ten days later, God fulfilled my desire. I was pregnant! I knew that if I trusted in God, he would provide me with another baby.

Six weeks later, things began to take a turn for the worst. We had our first ultrasound to measure the baby's heart rate. The doctors wanted the speed to be at least one hundred beats per minute. Our baby's heart was pumping—but at only fifty beats per minute. A miscarriage was most likely going to occur. We were devastated.

That night, I had a dream. In that dream, I saw a little girl with red, curly hair, pale skin, and a lot of freckles. She was around the age of six. Over and over again, she assured me that she was going to be okay. She told me that she was happy and that we would meet in heaven. She said that she loved me and that her name was Joy. I woke up suddenly and knew I was no longer pregnant. At six weeks and four days, my little girl had gone to be with Jesus. Ironically, or by the grace of God, my husband had experienced the same dream.

My heart was breaking. I took comfort in the fact that God provided the closure of that dream, but I was confused. What happened to my heart's desire? Nothing is impossible with God, so why did he not strengthen my baby's heart rate? Why did he allow my baby to die? What if I had listened to that voice? Had God been nudging me in a different direction to avoid heartbreak? Why did I not listen? Why did God not answer my prayer? He did answer my prayer. I was pregnant. I prayed that I would become pregnant, but I did not ask him for a healthy pregnancy. I did not ask for a live birth and a baby to hold in my arms. I was not specific enough, and God wants us to be specific. I vowed to myself that day that I would start praying specifically and that I would always listen to that unsettled feeling, that still small voice.

It was a hard time for me. I was depressed. I was in a dark hole and could not seem to get out of it. One in four women will experience a miscarriage.[20] What is hard about a miscarriage is that women are told not to share the news of pregnancy before twelve weeks, just in case. Most miscarriages happen very early in a pregnancy. So, because the announcement of pregnancy is not shared prior, women are stuck with putting on a fake smile and pretending that nothing happened. Women wonder if they did something wrong to cause this misfortune. A living person with a heartbeat and a unique set of DNA died. There is no visitation; there is no funeral. Women are dealing with this alone. I was alone, and the support given hurt more than helped. Phrases such as "At least you can get pregnant," "It will happen again," or "It was too early and not a real baby" can sting. My miscarriage was a baby, a loving child of God who I could picture playing on the playground and giving hugs and kisses to at night. I loved that child.

Death is hard. It is sad, but God gets it. God lost a child too.

His Son, Jesus, died. The Bible states that darkness covered the land for three hours after his immediate death. I knew God was mourning and weeping right alongside me. I found relief with a therapist who acknowledged that I had indeed experienced a loss. We created a memory box of cards and ultrasound pictures, and we even created a piece of jewelry to symbolize her presence in our lives. We named her Joy—or she told us her name—and I cannot wait to meet her in heaven!

Three months after our miscarriage, my husband received a job opportunity in St. Louis, Missouri, where we were both born and raised. It was the perfect time to move closer to family and friends and to heal. We felt very blessed. We had our three-year-old twin girls, had recently purchased a house in our hometown, had our health, and my husband had a job where I could stay at home, but I still felt like there was a missing piece to our family. The desire to have another baby did not stop after the miscarriage. Having a third baby became my obsession. It took over my life. I spent all of my time and energy thinking and talking about it.

I contemplated ways of fulfilling that need. I added my name to an adoption list. I had my husband take a woman's fertility drug, and I began saving for another round of IVF. I even had my daughters praying for a "baby in my belly." I could not enjoy the present situation and my current blessings. Proverbs tells us that four things will never satisfy us; those four things will consume us and become an obsession. An empty womb is one of those four things the Bible mentions. The Bible tells us that we must overcome our fixations. God should be our obsession.

> Jesus replied: "Love the Lord your God with all your heart and with all your soul and with all your mind." (Matthew 22:37).

It was hard when others asked if I was going to have another baby. I never knew what to say. I was in a place of childless couples and large families. I was under the umbrella of secondary infertility, and I wanted out of the club.

Secondary infertility affects more than three million women in the United States.[21] These couples have the joy of one child—but the heartbreak of not being able to conceive another. Doctors downplay this situation by telling couples to "keep trying." Those with secondary infertility usually receive less support from family and friends. Secondary infertility is very lonely.

During this time, I came across the story of Jesus healing the ten lepers. After the miraculous healing of Jesus, nine of the men immediately forgot to thank him. Only one returned his healing with gratitude. Only one remembered to say thank you. Was I becoming too entangled in my wants and needs that I forgot that God had provided my miracle twin babies? Did I forget the blessings of my daughters? Did I remember to thank God?

The desire to have a child is a God-given desire. He gave it to me, and because he gave it to me, he promises to comfort me when things do not go exactly as I had hoped and planned.

> Let us throw off everything that hinders and the sin that so easily entangles. And let us run with perseverance the race marked out for us, fixing our eyes on Jesus, the pioneer and perfecter of faith. (Hebrews 12:1–2)

I began to move past my obsession. I started to look at what God had provided. During that time, I found out my husband's new insurance covered an IVF cycle. We were elated! We decided that we were going to pursue IVF again. The unsettled feeling I had experienced before came back immediately. Even though I desperately wanted another child, I was not at peace with another round of IVF. According to doctors, IVF was our only option to conceive. Even if I was not at peace, we had to move forward. I ignored the feeling of unrest again.

I took my first dose of IVF medication in April 2013, the same day as my weekly Bible study. It was the story of Judah and Tamar. Judah was the son of Jacob. He had three sons. The oldest son married Tamar. He died and left Tamar childless. It was custom at that time for Tamar to marry the next son in line so that she could have a child. Those two sons were not men of God. They found ways to avoid conceiving a child with Tamar. God killed them. What did Tamar do next? She prostituted herself and slept with her father-in-law, Judah.

Most Bible scholars believe Tamar was desperate to be part of this family heritage, Jesus's line, but God opened my eyes to something completely different. I observed a woman who was aging and did not have a husband or a child. She was desperate for a child. She tried everything, including sleeping with her father-in-law. She did not have faith that God would provide her with offspring. Was I doing the same thing? Was I controlling the outcome instead of letting God be God?

The still small voice was getting louder. I prayed. I asked God to show me directly what he wanted. My Life Application Study Bible fell open to Luke 1:36-37 NLT:

> What's more, your relative Elizabeth has become pregnant in her old age! People used to say she was barren, but she has conceived a son and is now in her sixth month. For nothing is impossible with God.

Immediately after reading that verse, my husband called and shared that he too was unsure of this fertility treatment. He went on to share that nothing is impossible with God. We canceled the treatment. A sense of peace came over me immediately. The burden lifted. I no longer had that unsettled feeling.

I still wanted another baby, but I knew IVF was not what God wanted. We decided to stop all talk about a third child for one calendar year. For one year, there would be no mention of fertility treatments, no researching information on adoption, and no putting our names on an embryo adoption list. Nothing. Absolutely nothing. It was hard. Just because we stopped pursuing treatments did not mean that my heart changed. How were we going to conceive another child when doctors told us that we had less than a 1 percent chance of conceiving on our own?

In the next few months, life got busy for our family of four. We sold our home, moved back to Colorado, and started new jobs. My monthly cycle was late. No big deal. With all the stress of moving, it was expected. Often when I am "late," I take a home pregnancy test—and my cycle begins the very next day. I took the test, and the test showed a positive result: two lines. I scrambled for another test: "Pregnant." Nothing is impossible with God!

A few weeks later, I went to the doctor for an ultrasound and heard the baby's heartbeat. I could not believe it. The doctors had told us that we had less than a 1 percent chance of conceiving on our own. God does not deal with percentages. God is the same yesterday, today, and forever. On May 22, 2014, one year later— when my husband and I planned to resume the discussion of a third child—we welcomed Saul Matthew into the world. Saul means "desired" and "prayed for," and Matthew means "a gift from God." My impossible situation turned into a reality!

Infertility is a tough road that affects one in eight couples,[22] yet it is a very private topic. No one talks about it. No one knows. Appearance was more important than sharing a hardship. We wanted to give the impression that our marriage was perfect, that we were choosing to postpone children. After the twins were born, we continued to keep our infertility woes under wraps. There were ample times to explain our difficulties with conceiving. We were asked regularly if twins ran in the family. Still, we kept our fertility procedures to ourselves. When I experienced my miscarriage, I started sharing. I was finally gutsy enough to speak out.

To my amazement, no one judged us. Not one person

questioned us about our decisions. The complete opposite happened. Others started sharing their failed pregnancy attempts, their miscarriages, and their personal fertility stories. The more people I told, the better I felt. I realized that many couples are battling hardships and that God is using our infertility story to help others with theirs.

God created us to love one another just as he loves us. He wants us to call on him when we are in need. He also gives us people in our lives at the right time to help us on our life journeys.

A friend loves at all times, and a brother is born for a time of adversity. (Proverbs 17:17)

Be gutsy, be courageous, and go first. Share your story and lead the way. Step out in faith, knowing that God will hold your hand.

God knows our futures. He knows our whole story, and a little hiccup in the road can lead to an even bigger expectation like it did for us. We never expected twins. We never expected to become pregnant on our own after seven years of trying. We never expected to be holding our baby after the doctors told us we had less than a 1 percent chance of conceiving naturally, but it did happen. God expected it.

God tells us that life is not going to be easy. We will experience valleys. We will experience hardships and heartaches, but God also promises that if we follow him, he will guide our path. His light will shine forth. It will be a light that others will see. Throughout my infertility journey, I learned to be still and follow God's voice. I learned to trust in the Lord with all of my heart. I learned that God wants to hear my specific prayers. I learned that he is in control and will give you the desire of your heart in his timing and his way. Finally, I learned that God could do all things. Nothing is impossible with him.

Answered Prayers

ANSWERED PRAYERS

NOTES

1   "What is Infertility?," American Pregnancy Association, last modified July 27, 2017, accessed July 27, 2017, http://www.americanpregnancy. org/infertility/what-is-infertility.

2   Livingston, Gretchen and Cohn, D'Vera, *The New Demography of American Motherhood*, www.pewsocialtrends.org/2010/05/06/the-new-demography-of-american-motherhood/ (Published May 6, 2010).

3   Mascarella, Janene, *The Benefits of Older Parents*, https://www. parenting.com/article/older-parents (Accessed March 28, 2018).

4   Scriven, Joseph. "What a Friend We Have in Jesus." *Lutheran Worship*, 1886.

5   Disputed Author. *Footprints in the Sand*. (First published 1936).

6   Young, Sara. *Jesus Calling*. (Nashville: Thomas Nelson, 2004).

7   "Tips for Handling Holidays," https://resolve.org/support-managing-infertility-stress/ (Accessed March 28, 2018).

8   Robbins, Dale, *How to Make Godly Decisions*, www.victorious.org/pub/ godly-decisions-108 (Accessed March 28, 2018).

9   Adoption Exchange Association, "About the Children." https://www. adoptuskids.org/meet-the-children/children-in-foster-care/about-the-children (Accessed March 28, 2018).

10 Shanks, Pete, "How Many Embryos Are Left Over?" https://www. geneticsandsociety.org/biopolitical-times/how-many-embryos-are-left-over (Published October 8, 2008).

11 Boatner, Edward. "He's Got the Whole World in his Hands." *Spirituals Triumphant, Old and New,* (Nashville: Sunday School Publishing Board, 1927).

12 Keller, Timothy. *Prayer: Experiencing Awe and Intimacy with God.* (London: Penguin Books, 2016).

13 *My Best Friend's Wedding.* Director P. J. Hogan. Performer Rupert Everett. Zucker Brothers Productions, 1997. DVD

14 Miscarriage Statistics, https://www.tommys.org/our-organisation/charity-research/pregnancy-statistics/miscarriage (Accessed March 29, 2018).

15 Fast Facts, https://resolve.org/infertility-101/what-is-infertility/fast-facts/ (Accessed March 29, 2018).

16 RMA of Philadelphia, "Secondary Infertility Causes, Treatments & Emotional Effects," https://rmaspecialists.com/secondary-infertility/ (Published June 16, 2017).

17 Musco, Penny Schlaf, "When You Can't Conceive Again," www.todayschristianwoman.com/articles/2001/march/10.66.html (Accessed March 20, 2018).

18 Gann, Judy. *God of All Comfort.* (Chattanooga: Living Ink Books, 2005).

19 Chapman, Steven Curtis. "The Great Adventure." *The Great Adventure,* Sparrow Records, 1992.

20 Miscarriage Statistics, https://www.tommys.org/our-organisation/charity-research/pregnancy-statistics/miscarriage (Accessed March 29, 2018).

21 RMA of Philadelphia, "Secondary Infertility Causes, Treatments & Emotional Effects," https://rmaspecialists.com/secondary-infertiity/ (Published June 16, 2017).

22 "Fast Facts," https://resolve.org/infertility-101/what-is-infertility/fast-facts/ (Accessed March 29, 2018).

Printed in the United States
By Bookmasters